F-84 THUNDERJET
UNITS OVER KOREA

OSPREY FRONTLINE COLOUR

3

F-84 THUNDERJET UNITS OVER KOREA

Warren Thompson

First published in Great Britain in 2000 by Osprey Publishing
Elms Court, Chapel Way, Botley, Oxford, OX2 9LP, UK
E-mail: info@ospreypublishing.com

ISBN 1 84176 022 6

Edited by Tony Holmes
Page design by Ken Vail Graphic Design, Cambridge, UK
Cutaway Drawing by Mike Badrocke
Origination by Grasmere Digital Imaging, Leeds, UK
Printed in Hong Kong through Bookbuilders

00 01 02 03 04 05   10 9 8 7 6 5 4 3 2 1

EDITOR'S NOTE

To make the Osprey Frontline Colour series as authoritative as possible, the editor would be interested in hearing from any individual who may have relevant information relating to the aircraft/units/pilots featured in this, or any other, volume published by Osprey Aviation. Similarly, comments on the editorial content of this book would also be most welcome. Please write to Tony Holmes at 10 Prospect Road, Sevenoaks, Kent, TN13 3UA, Great Britain, or by e-mail at tony.holmes@osprey-jets.freeserve.co.uk

FOR A CATALOGUE OF ALL TITLES PUBLISHED BY OSPREY MILITARY, AUTOMOTIVE AND AVIATION PLEASE WRITE TO:

The Marketing Manager, Osprey Direct, PO Box 140, Wellingborough, Northants NN8 4ZA, United Kingdom
Email: info@ospreydirect.co.uk

Or visit us at: **www.ospreypublishing.com**

FRONT COVER *On 31 January 1951 the 27th Fighter Escort Wing (FEW) was pulled out of Taegu AB and moved back to Itazuke AB, in Japan. Although the latter site offered vastly improved accommodation and servicing facilities for the wing, the trade off was greatly increased flying time (which included the dreaded return water crossing of the Sea of Japan) to the frontlines. The wing would operate from this base until they were relieved by the 136th Fighter Bomber Group (FBG) in May of that same year. This photograph was taken by Mustang pilot Lt Roy Bell of the 18th FBG at Itazuke in the early spring of 1951, and shows a 522nd FES F-84E heading a line up of similarly-marked Thunderjets from the same unit. The squadron appears to have used both orange and red paint when applying its colours to these aircraft, whilst a close examination of the fin tip of FS-427 also reveals the yellow of the 523rd FEW, to whom this particular Thunderjet had been previously assigned (Roy Bell)*

BACK COVER *Lt Malcolm Pearson poses in the cockpit of his F-84 prior to flying his 125th, and final, mission over North Korea in 1953. Twenty-five of these sorties had been completed in F-80Cs, whilst the remainder were flown in Thunderjets with the 430th FBS/474th FBG from Kunsan and Taegu ABs. Remaining in the USAF following the completion of his tour, Pearson saw further action at the controls of a Republic fighter just over a decade later when he flew F-105D/F Thunderchiefs over both North and South Vietnam (Malcolm Pearson)*

TITLE PAGE *Groundcrews from the 27th FEW oversee the loading of their Thunderjets onto the flightdeck of the light aircraft carrier USS Bataan (CVL 29) at Naval Air Station North Island, in San Diego, in November 1950. Not enough time was spent preparing these aircraft for the trip across the Pacific, for most of them were found to have suffered varying degrees of salt water corrosion upon their arrival in the Far East. The resulting rectification work delayed the wing's introduction to combat by about a week. By mid-1951 the many carrier loads of aircraft that were being shipped over to Korea were well protected, and few suffered such corrosion damage as had been inflicted upon the F-86As of the 4th FIW and the F-84s of the 27th FEW in late 1950 (Wilbur Segerson)*

TITLE VERSO PAGE *429th FBS Commander, Maj 'Pappy' Hayes, spends time out on the flightline with some of his enlisted men as they prepare for the launch of the afternoon mission from Kunsan AB in early 1953. The two blue horizontal bands on the tail of this Thunderjet indicate its allegiance to Hayes' squadron within the 474th FBG (Bill Oliphant)*

Contents

LEFT *Ably assisted by his crew chief, Lt Gene Rohr straps into the cockpit of his 311th FBS/58th FBW Thunderjet at Taegu AB in 1953. With the number of aircrew on a squadron at any given time far exceeding the number of aircraft that was allocated to the unit, it was common practice for several pilots to fly missions in several different aircraft. In this instance, according to the titling on the canopy framing, Rohr is flying an F-84 assigned to a Lt A R McGowan (Gene Rohr)*

INTRODUCTION

Long before World War 2 ended, most of the major military powers were heavily involved in the research and development of jet-propelled aircraft. The Germans held a distinct advantage in this area over the United States and Great Britain, with Messerschmitt's Me 262 twin-engined fighter being easily the best jet-powered aircraft to see operational service during the conflict.

Both sides in that war realised that speed was not only life, but that it also meant power and victory. In the United States, most of the major aircraft manufacturers had jet-powered prototypes in the making, including Lockheed, Bell, North American and Republic.

By the time the latter company's effort in the shape of the XP-84 had flown in February 1946, the war had been over for almost six months. Nevertheless, the Army Air Force (AAF) still expressed a keen interest in the airframe. Republic lagged quite some distance behind both Bell and Lockheed, whose designs – the P-59 Airacomet and P-80 Shooting Star respectively – had already entered production. Indeed, the latter aircraft would go on to become the first truly successful frontline American jet fighter, and its service in Korea will be examined in detail in a later volume within this series.

The Shooting Star was a fighter interceptor which could trace its ancestry back to Lockheed's war-winning P-38 Lightning. And although capable of carrying up to 2000 lbs of bombs or rockets, it was hardly the tactical 'bomb truck' that the AAF felt it would need for any future conflict. This was where Republic came in, for the Long Island-based company had firmly established itself during World War 2 as *the* primary source of land-based close air support aircraft for the AAF, building no less than 15,683 P-47 Thunderbolts.

This rugged fighter-bomber had found employment across the globe, and provided the basis for Republic's jet-powered replacement, the F-84 Thunderjet. The design philosophy behind the P-47 also influenced the layout of the F-84's successor, the F-105 Thunderchief.

All three designs became famous during the course of three wars fought over three separate decades. Incredible physical strength was a trait common to all Republic aircraft, the P-47 proving capable of absorbing considerable damage from either flak emplacements or fighters. The F-84 exhibited similar tendencies during the Korean War, being regularly exposed to intense communist ground fire whilst 'mud-moving' in the demanding ground support role. For many of the pilots that flew the Thunderjet in combat, the jet's greatest attribute was its ability to absorb 'Triple-A', and still make it back to base. Republic's reputation for building 'survivable' fighter-bombers was further enhanced with the F-105 a little over a decade later in Vietnam.

Returning to the F-84, if this aircraft had any weaknesses, it had to be the fact that it was grossly underpowered. The fighter was fitted with a J35 axial-flow turbojet engine manufactured by Allison, who took an inordinately long time to improve the levels of thrust available from this powerplant. Indeed, the prolonged gestation of the design from XP-84 prototype to P-84B (redesignated F-84B on 11 June 1948) frontline fighter was so protracted that its straight-winged layout was considered obsolescent by the time the first examples were issued to the USAF's 14th Fighter Group (FG) at Dow Field, Maine, in November 1947. Numerous other jet fighter prototypes had begun to appear across the globe boasting refined aerodynamics, swept wings and more powerful engines.

Despite its lengthy development, the B-model Thunderjet was not considered easy to handle by its pilots due to its poor power response. Although the follow-on F-84C boasted improved levels of thrust thanks to its J35-A-13 engine, it was not until the arrival of the J35-A-17D-powered F-84D in November 1948 that the USAF at last had a suitable airframe/powerplant combination to perform the fighter-bomber role.

The outdated Bravo and Charlie model Thunderjets soon disappeared from the frontline force, and the USAF concentrated on purchasing 154 F-84Ds. The design was further improved with the advent of the F-84E, of which 743 were built for both the USAF and allied air forces, followed by the definitive G-model. No fewer than 3025 examples of the latter-model Thunderjet were constructed by Republic, although 'only' 1125 of these were supplied to the USAF (from August 1951).

Equipped with more powerful versions of the J35 engine, Jet-Assisted Take-Off (JATO) booster rockets, improved avionics and a greater bombload, the final two variants of the Thunderjet family would perform the bulk of the USAF's tactical bombing missions during the Korean conflict.

Warren E Thompson
Germantown, Tennessee
March 2000

OPPOSITE *Looking down the 'business end' of a Thunderjet. This was the same view that communist troops and truck drivers saw for much of the Korean War. The sheer volume of sorties flown by the F-84 can be gauged by the following statistics for the 49th FBG during the first six months of 1952. The group flew 6043 combat sorties and expended more than one million rounds of 0.50-cal ammunition. This Thunderjet was one of the aircraft flown by the 49th FBG's 7th FBS during this period (Ken Jackson)*

CHAPTER ONE

THE THUNDERJET'S DEBUT

The North Korean People's Army invaded South Korea on 25 June 1950. This would prove to be the first test of the United Nations' (UN) resolve to stop the spread of communism. It could not have come at a worse time, for the military powers of the free world had let their respective armed forces deteriorate to a fraction of the size of what they had been five years earlier. For example, the United States' military presence in the Far East was pitiful. Needless to say, the invaders from the north met with very little resistance from the US Army units that had been thrown in their path in an effort to slow them down. Indeed, it was not until a few weeks later that 'beefed up' Fifth Air Force assets began to finally make a dent in the North Korean efforts, allowing the ground troops to regroup.

With the success of the Inchon landings, and the North Koreans in retreat to the north, it appeared that Commander-in-Chief, Far East, Gen Douglas MacArthur, had 'pulled the rabbit out of the hat' – but not so! The overall pattern of the war did not become clear until the 'trump card' had been 'played' by the North Koreans in the shape of the Communist Chinese Army.

Two key things happened in November 1950 that would greatly effect the USAF, and the future way it did business. First of all, the Chinese entered the war in great numbers, turning the UN advance into retreat. This triggered the realisation that effective close air support was being delivered by vintage World War 2-type aircraft, and that the Navy's F9F and the Air Force's F-80 were not going to be able to handle the escalating workload.

ENTER THE MiG

Secondly, to compound this problem further, an all-silver, swept-wing 'bolt of greased lightning' in the shape of the Soviet-built MiG-15 made an unexpected appearance south of the Yalu River. Within days, the dream of being home for Christmas evaporated, and UN troops were once again reeling in the face of an overwhelming

communist onslaught. Trying to protect the withdrawal of ground forces hastily retreating south proved to be a hellish job for the handful of fighter-bomber units in-theatre. The brunt of this effort was performed by pilots flying the old 'war horses' from World War 2 in the shape of the USAF's F-51 Mustang and the Marine Corps' F4U Corsair. Both types were the only combat aircraft capable of operating from crude North Korean bases, which gave them immediate access to enemy troop positions and supply lines. They flew from dawn to dusk, seven days a week, and never let up.

Far East Air Force's (FEAF) High Command was dealing with trying to stop a million Chinese troops, and this crucial battle would have to be fought against the backdrop of a typically bitter Korean winter. The first order of business was to close up some of the gaps in the fighter-bomber's coverage of the frontline, and deal with potential problem areas before they became mission critical – both aspects that would require long term solutions. This meant getting the authorisation to bring the Republic F-84 Thunderjet and the North American F-86 Sabre into the Korean Theatre of Operations, and USAF Chief of Staff, Gen Hoyt Vandenburg, duly granted FEAF's requests in early November.

It might interest the reader to know that the earlier models of F-84 were slated to replace the F-80s in Japan sometime in mid-1949. This never happened, however, due to the fact that most of the airfields in Japan were considered too short to handle the fighter-bomber. Had this plan been carried out, the FEAF would have boasted

at least three full fighter-bomber wings of Thunderjets in Japan and perhaps a single wing on Okinawa.

Although the F-84 was designed as a fighter, the F-86 soon proved itself far superior in this role. The latter type would have a better chance of protecting both piston-engined and jet-powered fighter-bombers from marauding MiGs. The F-84 would be left to make its mark in the air-to-ground role, carrying a significant warload of bombs and rockets over greater distances than any other fighter-bomber in Korea. Its arrival in-theatre at last meant that the FEAF could hammer key targets along the length of the Yalu River. Working closely with each other, the Thunderjet and Sabre would be tasked with implementing the Fifth Air Force's new interdiction strategy for North Korea, which was still in its infancy in early 1951.

The Pentagon decision makers had chosen the 'Just Famous' gang from the 27th Fighter Escort Wing (FEW) to debut the new F-84E in battle. This outfit was one of the most elite within the Strategic Air Command (SAC) organisation, having been previously selected to escort B-29s and B-50s into the Soviet Union should World War 3 have erupted in the late 1940s. The wing was initially equipped with the F-51D, but quickly transitioned to the 'long-legged' F-82E Twin Mustang. It was with these impressive interceptors that the 27th FEW completed the numerous long distance overwater formation flights in support of SAC bombers that made it legendary within the USAF.

The 27th's pilot roster read like something out of a 'Who's Who in the Air Force', with 60 per cent of its avia-

ABOVE This is a good side view of the F-84E assigned to 522nd FES CO, Lt Col William Bertram, upon his arrival in Korea. Seen here loaded up with 500-lb General-Purpose (GP) bombs, the aircraft is leading out two other Thunderjets from the squadron's open air dispersal at Taegu AB in December 1950. This photograph was taken soon after the Chinese had entered the war, and when all the fighter-bombers based on Korean soil were utilising every minute of daylight to bomb the enemy forces. Col Bertram's claim to fame was that he 'bagged' the first MiG-15 to fall to the F-84 in Korea following an engagement on 21 January 1951 (Don Watt)

tors having experienced fighter combat during World War 2.

Above all, the 27th FEW loved to fly, and for the previous four years of its existence in SAC, had been allocated more flying time than just about any other fighter organisation in the USAF. Much of this had to do with the top priority given to any SAC unit at the time. And the wing was also a classic example of the old heads teaching the new ones, for the younger pilots that had joined the 27th straight out of jet training benefited greatly from the operational guidance of wartime pilots. All these positive points combined to make the 27th FEW the obvious choice for the Korean mission.

The arrival of the F-84 in the Far East in December 1950 initially created more excitement than had been aroused by the debut of the F-86 the previous month. This was due to the fact that the Chinese Army had already committed itself, and the threat it posed to the UN troops at the front was real. The MiGs, on the other hand, had yet to make any real impression on fighter-bomber operations, or friendly ground troops, south of the Yalu. Of course, this latter situation had drastically changed by mid-January 1951 to the point where the FEAF was demanding more than the one wing of F-86s then in-theatre.

COMBAT DEBUT

The Fifth Air Force had initially wanted to base the 27th FEW at Kimpo AB (K-14) in order for the wing to be close to the frontline, but by the time the jets arrived in Japan, the situation had deteriorated so badly that the Thunderjets ended up further south at Taegu AB (K-2) instead. A first class rear maintenance facility was simultaneously set up at Itazuke AB, in Japan.

With Chinese troops streaming south, the firepower of the F-84 was desperately needed, and the wing made its combat debut on 6 December 1950. Led by World War 2 ace Col Don Blakeslee, the F-84 pilots were tasked with flying an armed reconnaissance mission southwest of Pyongyang. They were teamed up with the battle-weary 49th Fighter Bomber Group (FBG), who also flew from Taegu in F-80Cs. Needless to say, targets were plentiful due to their flightpath intersecting the enemy's main supply route (MSR) toward the 38th Parallel, which was feeding the North Korean Army's rapid advances to the south.

The three flights of F-84s sent on this inaugural mission fired off all their ordnance and ammunition (which consisted of 32 rockets and 7200 rounds of 0.50-cal), hitting a rail marshalling yard and disabling several locomotives. As the pilots turned and headed south once again, they stuck firmly to the roads, strafing anything that moved until they had finally exhausted their magazines.

The number of moving targets they encountered gave them ample excuse to expend the rest of their ammunition, and several secondary explosions were spotted. The first mission had been a great success, and the enemy was left in little doubt as to the effectiveness of the F-84.

Over the next 30 days, the 27th FEW flew 927 effective sorties, totalling more than 1800 hours of cockpit time. According to their records, the breakdown of mission types was as follows – 275 close support, 525 armed reconnaissance and 75 escorts. By war's end in 1953, these figures would be well and truly overshadowed by the feats of the newer F-84 groups in Korea, but these early statistics of the pioneer Thunderjet wing carry more meaning than at first meets the eye.

The 27th FEW was a fighter escort organisation that had always specialised in air-to-air combat. It had been pulled out of this role at short notice and thrown into a war where the air-to-ground mission was the primary assignment. For most units, this fundamental role change would have meant a cautious transition over a matter of weeks. However, with communist forces on the verge of ejecting UN troops from Korea for good in December 1950, the 27th had little choice but to perform the close air support mission within days of arriving in-theatre. And thanks to the combination of experienced pilots flying the right aircraft type, the wing not only tackled the air-to-ground tasking head on, it excelled at it.

OPPOSITE ABOVE When the temperature got warmer, or when flying from shorter runways, the heavily-loaded F-84s had trouble getting off the ground. To overcome these problems the units regularly resorted to fitting JATO (Jet-Assisted Take Off) bottles to the underside of the Thunderjet, which proved a spectacular success. These particular aircraft were assigned to the 522nd FES

OPPOSITE BELOW A 524th FES Thunderjet returns storeless, having completed its mission. These aircraft used Taegu AB for just seven weeks before moving to Japan. The 27th had retained a major presence at Itazuke, having left most of its Wing HQ and maintenance personnel in Japan when it initially moved to South Korea. By utilising assembly line techniques for maintenance at its rear base, the wing was able to keep most of its 48 aircraft in commission. The adoption of this practice proved to be a major boon for the FEAF as its units flew round-the-clock in an effort to stop the Chinese offensive (Allen Nelson)

One of the 524th FES's F-84Es taxies down the runway after landing back at Taegu following the completion of a short mission over the frontline in December 1950. The assigned identification colours for the three squadrons within the 27th FEW were as follows: red for the 522nd, yellow for the 523rd and blue for the 524th. Although the wing was temporarily attached to the FEAF whilst in Korea, it still technically belonged to SAC (Allen Nelson)

CHAPTER TWO

THUNDERJET NUMBERS INCREASE

During the first few months of 1951, the impact that the recently-arrived F-84 had on the war was phenomenal. Although there were only three squadrons in-theatre, the 48 aircraft that they controlled ranged all over North Korea dropping napalm and general-purpose bombs, and firing rockets. And despite the escalation of the MiG-15 threat in February and March, the Thunderjets also proved far more capable of taking care of themselves than either the F-80 or the F-51.

Yet, despite proving a success in combat, the 27th FEW was moved to Itazuke, in Japan, after just two months in Korea. This decision was taken by FEAF HQ following the overcrowding of the modest Taegu facility with units that had retreated from bases further north. There simply wasn't enough room for all three squadrons to operate from the airfield. Although now a greater distance from the action, the F-84E took the base move in its stride thanks to its legendary 'long legs', which made flights into North Korea from Japan a realistic proposition.

The 27th FEW launched its last missions out of Taegu on 31 January, and the following day commenced combat operations from Itazuke, where it would remain until replaced by the 136th Fighter Bomber Group (FBG) in May of that year.

During the wing's 60-day Taegu tour, the F-84s had been operating pretty much on their own, as they ventured way up into the extreme north-western corner of North Korea to deliver their bombs. In the spring of 1951, this area became world famous as 'MiG Alley' following numerous clashes between 4th Fighter Interceptor Wing (FIW) F-86s and communist MiG-15s.

Due to the increased MiG activity, the 4th FIW often had to spread its Sabre force so thinly that it could not cover all the fighter-bomber missions that were being carried out in this vast area. This meant that F-84 pilots would have to fend for themselves, and they relished the opportunity to engage the MiGs.

Indeed, If you were to study all of the statistics that came out of the Korean War for the first six months of 1951, as impressive as those for the Thunderjet were in its air-to-ground role, it was in the demanding air-to-air arena that the jet excelled! The first five aerial kills (four of which were MiG-15s) in that year were credited to the 27th FEW. These figures only serve to reinforce the fact that pilots flying the F-84E soon mastered the art of aerial gunnery, which they had practiced when part of the peacetime SAC force.

The first kill of the new year was recorded on 21 January by Lt Col William Bertram, CO of the 522nd FES. His success came following two days of increased MiG activity south of the Yalu River, the communist pilots intent on breaking up the daily forays of the fighter-bombers. At

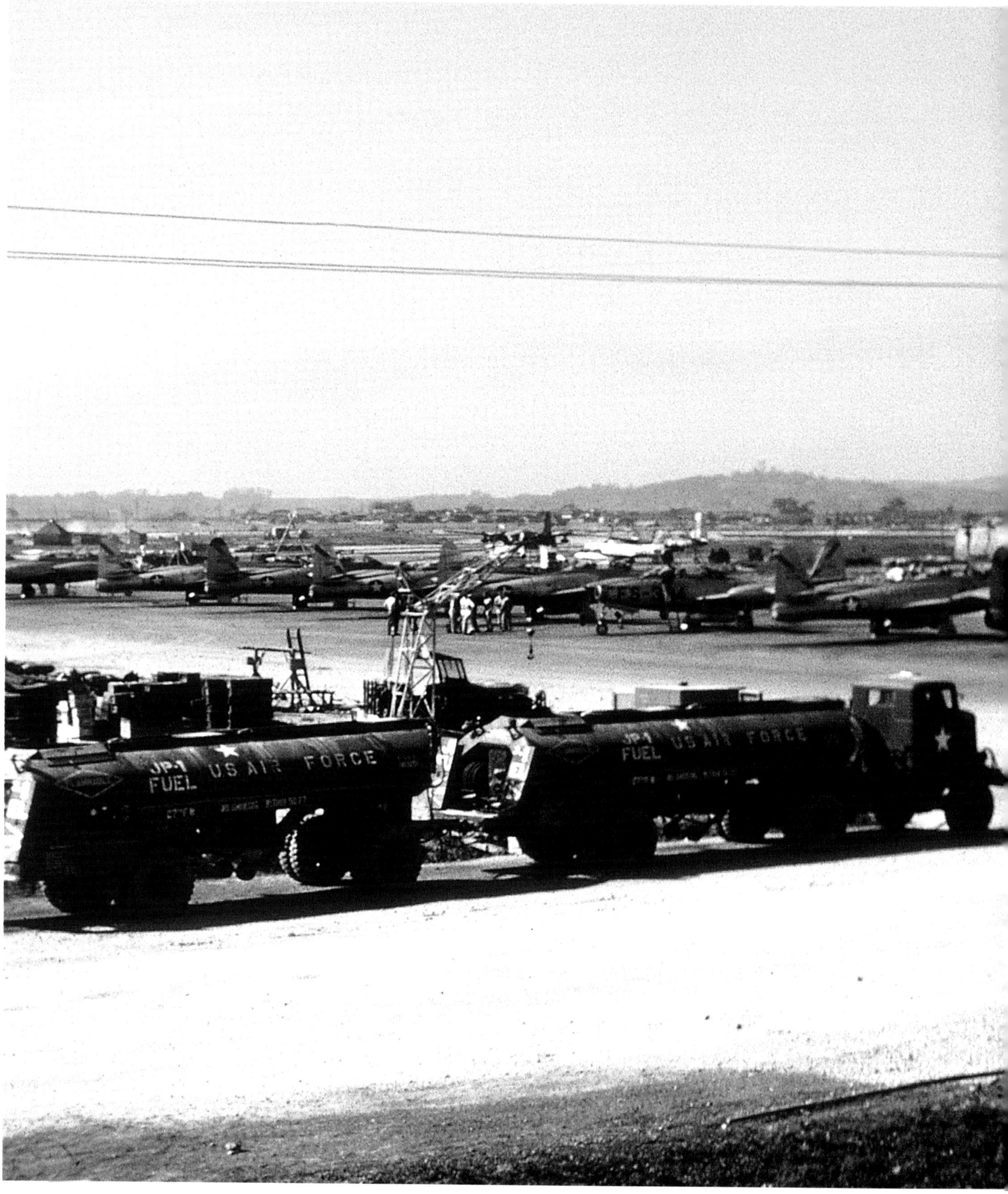
JP-1
FUEL US AIR FORCE
JP-1
FUEL US AIR FORCE

This view clearly shows just how crowded the flightline was at Itazuke shortly before the 27th FEW moved back to the USA. Note that all of the F-84s (from the 522nd FES) in shot have long-range centreline fuel tanks fitted. The 136th FBG began replacing the 27th on 1 June 1951, and by 1 August the transition had been completed. At about this time, the 49th FBG was also receiving F-84s, thus increasing the size of the Thunderjet force in-theatre to two complete groups (Don Watt)

ABOVE These 522nd FES F-84Es are seen parked at Taegu AB in the spring of 1951. At this stage in the war all Thunderjets involved in the fighting were based at Itazuke AB, so these two aircraft were probably photographed during a refuelling stop after completing their strike mission in North Korea. Note the mandatory external tanks attached to both jets (George Busher)

first the Soviet-built fighters simply sparred with the F-84s, racing back north whenever the USAF pilots tried to turn into them. However, by the 21st the communists had started to press home their attacks, and had thus become a genuine threat. The 27th FEW's Lt Don Watt was involved in the MiG 'killing' engagement;

'Our target for that morning was a double railroad bridge outside the city of Kwaksan, in north-west Korea. This area was only 50 miles from Antung (where MiG-15s were known to be based). We were a flight of 12 F-84Es, with eight of us carrying two 500-lb GP bombs and the remaining four aircraft flying as top cover. Due to all the MiG activity we had seen the day before, we were confident that we would bring them up again.

'None of us had had much experience in the F-84 when we moved into Korea. Only a few of the pilots had fired the guns on them, and none had dropped bombs. We learned fast!'

'Col William Bertram was leading the mission, and I was flying his wing. After joining up, we headed north-west toward out target, which was about one hour's flying time away. We passed another flight coming out of North Korea, and they informed us they had been jumped by MiGs, and told us to keep our eyes open. The remainder of the flight up to the target was uneventful, but this quickly changed once we had got there.

'Col Bertram found our target – a bridge – and I fell in trail behind him and we made a pass. Our remaining elements were stacked up with several thousand feet separating each of them. Just as I saw Bertram's bombs hit the bridge, our top cover called out that there were MiGs west of us over the water. I was on my second run and had just toggled my bombs when Lt Simpson, with our other element, yelled for his wingman to break left. He had been hit and another MiG was on the second F-84's tail. At this time, our other flight and our top cover had also been jumped

'There were MiGs everywhere, and one of our pilots later stated that they were so close that he could hear their cannons firing. Somewhere in this melee one of the enemy aircraft went down in flames. It had fallen victim to Col Bertram's guns. I broke off my dive-bomb run and followed the colonel into the sun. Up ahead, I saw one MiG start a gentle turn to the left, and I went after him at full throttle. My gunsight was on him and I was firing short bursts, even though he was out of range.

'I didn't know this at the time, but there was a MiG on my tail blazing away as well. Jake Kratt later told me that the MiG was so close that both it and my F-84 were in his sights, so he couldn't fire! Kratt radioed, "Whoever is in a big slow turn to the left had better break as he has one right behind him". I broke sharply left, hauled back on the stick and there was a sudden jar. Cold air began rushing all around me so I turned the cockpit heat up to "full". My goggles were also gone, but I still had my mask and helmet. I then pointed the nose of the jet down and headed for the deck, and it was only then that I realised that my canopy was gone! I pulled back on the throttle and stayed as close to the ground as I could so as to prevent a MiG from making a pass at me.

'I headed south, radioing for someone to join up with me, but no one was around. I noticed one F-84 in the distance as I passed Pyongyang, but he never saw me. I transmitted my position every five minutes, and later the guys on the other end said they had to turn up the heat in their cockpits to knock off the chill that my voice gave them! Most of the wind came in around the windscreen and tugged at my shoulders and back. I levelled off at 27,000 ft and the temperature outside was -45°F. I was met by Lt Bill Manahan about 60 miles from the base, and he escorted me all the way in. It had been a long day for the 27th, but we had made our first "kill" of the war!'

KRATT COMBAT

One of the most impressive fights with the MiGs was recorded just 48 hours later on 23 January by 1Lt Jake Kratt of the 523rd FES. He 'bagged' two jets in a single mission, which was undoubtedly the greatest aerial achievement by an F-84 pilot in Korea. Here, Lt Kratt recalls the details of the sortie;

'On this day, we were going after the big airfield up at Sinuiju, which was right on the Yalu, and only about 15 miles from the MiG base at Antung.

'Our mission leader was Col Don Blakeslee. The plan was to load all of the aircraft from the 522nd and 524th FESs with frag bombs and 5-in rockets. Their objective was to destroy the hangers and any parked aircraft. The 523rd was given the task of providing top cover during the mission. My flight position was element lead, with my old buddy Forrest Wilson on my wing.

'It was exceptionally cold and crystal clear as we formed up and headed for the target. We took up our positions and there was no radio chatter. During my normal scan for enemy aircraft, I noted that the sun was positioned at our four o'clock, and perhaps 40 degrees above the horizon. As we approached Sinuiju, I could see dust plumes billowing from the airfield over at Antung, and assumed that the MiGs were taking off. My hunch was correct. A couple of minutes later I saw a flash – a reflection of an object, then eight or nine more. These were identified as MiGs directly over the river at about 2500 ft. They were at full power and heading east towards

BELOW *Conducting an armed reconnaissance mission over North Korea was a dangerous business due to the low altitudes at which the F-84 pilots flew. Having been damaged by intense ground fire from a truck convoy during just such a mission, this 524th FES Thunderjet suffered a collapsed nose gear upon landing. Fortunately for the pilot, the rain-soaked ground surrounding the runway reduced the level of damage inflicted on the aircraft. This photograph was taken in the early spring of 1951 (Francis Clark)*

our target area. I called the MiGs to my leader, who did not acquire them immediately.

'Concurrently, the first flights had just begun their runs at the target, so there was no time to spare, as they would be easy pickings for the enemy fighters. My wingman and I began our dive toward the MiG formation from 14,000 ft with speed brakes extended, idle power and red line indicated airspeed.

Our approach from the MiGs' point of view was at about two o'clock out of the sun. I initially planned to disrupt the formation and give our guys a better chance of completing their mission before engaging the bogeys. I was firing my guns on the way down, hoping perhaps for a lucky shot to distract them, but it didn't work. As luck would have it, our high side 5g approach brought us in about 2000 ft behind their formation. During this process, I retracted my brakes and ran engine power up to 100 per cent, and was perfectly aligned on the tailpipe of the MiG flight leader.

'I gave him two long bursts and could see the rounds impact in his tailpipe area. Smoke quickly began streaming out and he began a left turn over the river, only to crash. His wingman turned with him, but not before I was able to get a quick shot in. At this point, our overtake speed was such that we were well within 1000 ft of the remainder of the formation and closing at a good rate, so I elected to pull up to the right to see what opportuni-

ties might be presented thereafter. As you might imagine, the place turned into a beehive of activity.

'In our breakaway manoeuvre, Forrest Wilson and I suddenly found ourselves on the defensive as four MiG-15s, flying in elements of two, were expending their ammo at a great rate – all in our direction! We continued our climb and increased our turn radius to the point where they were losing the advantage, and they disengaged. Immediately after this, I spotted another flight directly beneath us at a much lower altitude. I began a vertical spiral until I was in a good position. We then performed a healthy pull-out, cleared out tails, and once again found ourselves beautifully aligned at a range of about 2000 ft. I fired several long bursts. It was almost identical to the first shoot down, with plenty of smoke streaming from the MiG until it crashed into the ground. It had been a great day, and all of our aircraft returned safely to Taegu.'

Lt Kratt's skilled demonstration of air-to-air tactics had produced two kills, but the day was not yet over for the 27th FEW. This time the 522nd would also claim a MiG-15, which fell to the guns of Capt William Slaughter, who remembers;

'For some reason or another I was not scheduled to fly my regular aircraft on this mission, instead being allocated an F-84 that had been "written up" as firing 200 ft low and to the left at a distance of 1000 ft – it had the

BELOW *The blue trim worn by these F-84Es denotes that they belong to the 111th FBS, which in peacetime was an ANG-manned squadron based in Houston, Texas. On 30 July 1951, the 111th flew its first mission deep into North Korea, the unit being accompanied on this occasion by a handful of combat veterans from the 524th FES. The latter pilots had stayed behind to help with the 111th's transition to wartime operations, and on 2 August the new unit began flying combat missions by itself (William Colgan)*

LEFT *Although based at Taegu, these F-84s from the 111th FBS are seen parked at Suwon in 1951. Note that only the aircraft closest to the camera has been adorned with the unit's traditional five-pointed star on the tail, the remaining fighters still carrying the markings they wore when flown by the 27th FEW. In the distant background can be seen both F-80Cs from the 8th FBG and Col Frank Gabreski's newly-arrived F-86Es of the 51st FIW (Dick Petercheff)*

ABOVE *Although this F-84 from 111th FBS appears to have suffered a direct flak hit, this damage was actually caused by an errant tip tank which struck the vertical stabiliser after being jettisoned by the pilot. This photograph was taken at Taegu AB in the late summer of 1951 (Bill Lippincott)*

makings of a very long day! The mission plan called for us to make a few strafing passes over the enemy airfield to lure the MiGs up from their base at Antung. On my first strafing pass I tried to mark an ''X'' on the windscreen with a grease pencil, indicating where my bullets hit, since I could not depend on the gunsight. To top it off, we had been told by the powers-that-be that we could not use tracer ammo because it was misleading.

'As we came across Sinuiju, we could see the MiGs taking off. It didn't take long to mix it up with them. Suddenly, two MiG-15s popped up into position from our four o'clock. It was about time for us to exit the area because the MiGs were much faster than we were. In fact, the only way to get a good shot at them was to let them make a pass at us and then try and pick them off as they went by.

'The two MiGs that were firing at us were pretty far out. I fired a short burst at the leader and did not observe any hits, but I must have found the target because he immediately popped his speed brakes in an attempt to make me slide by. I was able to close rapidly, with my wingman calling out that he would cover me. I fired

several short bursts from very close range, trying to guess where my guns were shooting. I finally got hits in the MiG's cockpit and wingroot area. After one long burst, he started trailing light smoke and went down in a shallow dive, with no evasive action. We were down to about 1500 ft, and I was sitting on his tail waiting to get a picture, when he hit the ground.

'My trance was broken when some big red golf balls appeared over my right shoulder and passed under my nose. It was then that I realised the second MiG had broken through my cover, so I broke hard right, hoping to evade him and reverse the situation. I called out to find out where my wingman, Billy Edens, was and he said he was in a fight high above me. As I looked up, I saw an aircraft coming straight down trailing flames, and I was afraid it might have been Edens.

'In a matter of seconds, I knew it wasn't him. Shortly after that we formed up, and with our fuel situation approaching critical, we headed back to our base at Taegu.'

After debriefing, it was concluded that the flaming MiG-15 that Slaughter had seen was actually one of Lt Kratt's kills.

MISSION PRIORITIES

The mission letter that was issued to the 27th FEW when it arrived in-theatre consisted of the following seven key points;

1 Destroy enemy airpower in the air or on the ground
2 Give close support to United Nations' ground forces
3 Make armed reconnaissance and offensive strikes
4 Interdict enemy ground lines of supply and communications
5 Provide escort or cover for UN air, sea or land forces
6 Provide air defence of military installations
7 Provide special missions as required

As the build up of F-84s and F-86s continued on into 1952, these points would undergo several fundamental changes. The Sabre would become the primary air superiority type and the F-94 Starfire all-weather fighter would take on much of the air defence tasking once sufficient numbers of the big Lockheed interceptor had arrived in Korea. This left the Republic-built 'heavy haulers' to concentrate on what they did best – bomb the enemy.

By late January 1951, the arrival of additional F-86s and F-94s was still many months away, and the 27th FEW would be left to deal with the MiGs alone. With four kills in three days, it could be argued that the wing hardly required any outside assistance! And its run of aerial success was not quite over yet either, for on 26 January 1Lt Kratt engaged a piston-engined Yak-3 fighter of the North Korean People's Air Force north of Pyongyang;

'Our mission that day called for the destruction of a rail bridge approximately 20 miles from the North Korean capital. This time the 523rd would hit the bridge while the other two squadrons provided top cover. Our planned tactic was to glide bomb with 1000-lb GPs fitted with 15-second delayed action fuses. The defences around the bridge were light and the weather was not a factor. It was during my bomb run that someone called out a prop-driven aircraft on the deck, heading for the bridge and firing his guns. I had just released my last bomb when I made a quick visual sweep in all directions and, much to my amazement, I saw this intruder about 500 ft in front of my windscreen going from my right to left.

'I immediately applied full power to assist in executing a maximum-g turn to the left. In the meantime, our mission leader stated that he wanted positive identification prior to any shooting taking place. My squadron commander identified the intruder as the enemy just as the second and third F-84s overshot due to excessive speed. In the meantime, I decided to reduce power and extended the speed brakes to bleed off speed. By the time the okay was given, I already had my gunsight pipper trained on the target, and I fired a long burst. The Yak immediately started burning, rolled inverted and dove into the ground about five miles north of Pyongyang. The bridge span was dropped into the water and all of our aircraft returned safely to Itazuke.'

MORE JETS REQUESTED

The aircraft most sort after by the FEAF for the Korean theatre were the F-84 and F-86, and production lines of both types back in the USA could not match the demand. Priorities, therefore, had to be set, and the defence of North America was considered to be most important, followed by the protection of western Europe as part of the USA's commitment to the North Atlantic Treaty

BELOW *These 9th FBS aircraft are seen parked at Taegu AB in the autumn of 1951. Nicknamed the 'Iron Knights', the unit began converting from the F-80C to the F-84 in the summer of 1951, its parent group (the 49th FBG) making the transition at about the same time as the 136th FBG was replacing the 27th FEW. Notice the 9th's T-33 'hack' parked at the end of the line, this aircraft being retained by the squadron long after it had relinquished the last of its F-80s (Arnold Braswell)*

Organisation (NATO). This meant that FEAF would not receive anywhere near the number of aircraft that they had requested.

However, to counter the increasing MiG threat, the FEAF received enough brand new F-86Es in late 1951 to allow the F-80C-equipped 51st FIW to convert onto the latest Sabre variant. Due to the heavy attrition rate suffered by the now obsolete Shooting Star, the 49th FBW had also replaced its Lockheed fighters with F-84Es, completing the conversion in July 1951.

This now put two full wings of Thunderjets in the skies over Korea, leaving the remaining F-80s to be funnelled into the 8th FBW at Suwon.

Prior to leaving Japan, pilots from the outgoing 27th FEW helped with the conversion of the 49th FBW and the theatre acclimatisation of the 136th FBW. Both units were declared operational by early August 1951.

On 20 July, Gen Vandenburg stated that there would be no more FEAF squadrons converted onto the F-84, and that the request for 50 per cent back up reserves would not be met – at best there would only be a ten per cent reserve of aircraft.

By mid-May 1951, UN intelligence sources had come up with some impressive figures relating to the Chinese presence in Korea. They determined that there were

approximately 60 Chinese divisions on the peninsula, with the majority of them within the frontline area. Each division needed a minimum of 40 tons of supplies per day to remain combat ready. This effectively meant that 2400 tons of supplies was being 'trained and trucked' south each day to maintain the status quo at the front. Should the Chinese decide to mount an offensive, this figure would increase significantly. Most, if not all, of these supplies were being moved under the cover of darkness.

The USAF had tasked two wings of F-84s and single wings of F-80s and F-51s with interrupting this flow of supplies through North Korea, pilots searching out camouflaged targets, severing railway lines and destroying key road junctions.

It was the publication of this intelligence data that led to the Pentagon's decision to send another Air National Guard (ANG) wing – the 116th FBW – to the Far East to 'bolster Japan's Air Defence'. In reality, the wing would act as a 'safety valve' in-theatre, helping to counter any sudden Chinese offensive.

136th FBG

When the 136th FBG was told that it was to replace the 27th FEW within the FEAF, the group's component squadrons were sharing the facilities at Langley AFB,

BELOW Any squadron that was based in Korea or Japan during the winter months experienced both the wrath of cold temperatures and plenty of snow. This blue-trimmed F-84E was flown by the 159th FBS out of Misawa, Japan, during the winter of 1951-52. Even in these extreme conditions, the 116th FBW succeeded in keeping most of its aircraft operational on a daily basis. This Thunderjet is being refuelled for a practice mission over Japan – note the fixed refuelling probe extending forward from the tip tank (Robert Mason)

Virginia, with regular USAF fighter units. Prior to being called up for active duty on 10 October 1950, the group's trio of squadrons – 111th, 154th and 182nd FBSs – had been flying F-51Ds from Little Rock, Arkansas (154th), and Houston (111th) and San Antonio (182nd), in Texas.

Coming together at Langley in late October, the group continued to fly Mustangs until issued with brand new F-84Es in March of the following year. Once fully converted onto the Thunderjet, the 136th departed for California on 11 May 1951, and then on to Itazuke.

Being an ANG outfit, a significant percentage of the group's personnel were World War 2 veterans with at least five years' of service in the forces. The deployment of the 136th into the frontline proved to be a far more emotional affair than if it had been a regular air force group that had been sent. Its 'troops' were all 'weekend warriors', with regular jobs and young families, and it was tough to see them go back into action just six years after World War 2 had ended.

The entire 136th FBG arrived at Itazuke on 17 May, and within 48 hours pilots were attending a pre-dawn briefing for their first combat mission over Korea. The aircraft flown on this inaugural operation were all from the 27th FEW, manned by a mixture of pilots from both wings. The following brief summary of that first mission is held in the 136th's official history records;

'The sky was overcast, ceiling 500 ft, tops of the overcast were at approximately 35,000 ft. The mission was one of close support on the frontlines, helping to drive the retreating enemy forces back up the Inje Valley. Our aircraft put numerous napalm bombs among the enemy troops. After expending all ordnance, the group headed back south over the overcast at 35,000 ft, homeward bound down the Korean Peninsula to cross the Straits of the Yellow Sea at Pusan, checking in with the air controllers at Itazuke, before hitting the Japanese coast. All aircraft returned safely.'

116th FBW

On 5 July 1951 the 116th FBW received word that it too would soon be posted to Japan on a tour of temporary duty, attached to the FEAF. At the time these orders were cut, the wing was expecting to be sent to Europe. However, UN intelligence indicated that the Chinese were threatening a new offensive in Korea, and additional F-84s would be needed to deal with this. Less than one

ABOVE 111th FBS pilot Lt Tom Ingrassia straps into his aircraft, with the help of his crew chief, at the start of yet another mission. Well-known within his unit, Ingrassia was later killed in a peacetime flying accident in 1962 (Charles Joseph)

week after receiving its orders, the 116th was ready to deploy. Between 10 and 12 July, the wing loaded all its aircraft and personnel onto the escort carriers USS *Sitkoh Bay* and USS *Wyndham Bay* for the trip to Japan. The jets were off-loaded at Yokosuka on 27 July, and the maintenance crews quickly got to work preparing the aircraft at Kisarazu for the short flight to their new base at Misawa.

The ANG-manned 116th FBW was comprised of three squadrons from three states, although they had all been brought together at George AFB, California, following activation in October 1950. Each unit was then equipped with F-80Cs, the 158th FBS flying in from Georgia, the 159th from Florida and the 196th from nearby Norton AFB, California. The first F-84Es flew into George in April 1951, and by the early summer the wing was deemed ready to be sent overseas.

As previously mentioned, upon its arrival in Japan the 116th FBG HQ, along with the 158th and 159th FBSs, was sent north to Misawa AB, whilst the 196th FBS initially operated by itself from Chitose AB, on nearby Hokkaido. An intense combat training programme for all three squadrons commenced during the first week of August.

49th FBG

Unlike the incoming ANG-manned F-84 groups, the 49th FBG had seen plenty of combat by the time it transi-

tioned to Thunderjets in the spring of 1951. Formed as the 49th Fighter Wing on F-51Ds at Misawa AB in August 1948, it had been assigned to the FEAF's Fifth Air Force. One of the first fighter bomber wings to answer the call to arms in Korea, the 49th's 7th ('Screaming Demons'), 8th ('Black Sheep') and 9th ('Iron Knights') FBSs made their combat debut in July 1950, flying F-80Cs from the Japanese mainland. Eventually, the wing moved closer to the action, flying firstly from Suwon and then Taegu.

The 7th and 8th FBSs were the first to begin training with the new Republic jet at Itazuke, while the 9th FBS continued to fly the wing's remaining F-80s from Taegu until it was time for their conversion. Few problems were encountered during the swap from Lockheed to Republic fighters thanks to the wealth of experience within the 49th – most pilots had already completed at least 50 missions apiece in the fighter-bomber role.

With the FEAF now reaching its peak strength for F-84s in 1951, the Thunderjets began to make their presence felt in North Korea. Indeed, there were days in the late summer and early autumn when all you could see was 'wall-to-wall' F-84s, protected by several flights of F-86 Sabres. They fighter-bombers pounded key communist targets along the south side of the Yalu River almost on a daily basis. Many of these missions were opposed by MiG-15s coming south from Antung and other bases in

OPPOSITE *Strapped in and ready to go, Lt J D Brown of the 182nd FBS sits in his cockpit ready to taxy out to the Taegu (K-2) runway. In September 1951, the 136th FBG, along with all of its supporting squadrons, moved from Japan to the Korean base. Following this relocation, both F-84 wings at last found themselves operating from the same airfield. For the 136th FBG, the move also meant that it was much closer to its targets in the north (J D Brown)*

LEFT *These yellow-trimmed Thunderjets belonged to the Taegu-based 8th FBS 'Black Sheep'. This photograph was taken in late 1951, when both the 49th and 136th FBWs were operating from the base. Most of the major maintenance was also performed at K-2, and these jets are seen having their 0.5-in machine guns serviced (Lynn Balow)*

Manchuria, the communist pilots trying to force the fighter-bombers to jettison their bombloads prematurely. Despite protection from F-86s, most F-84 pilots were jumped at least once by a MiG-15. When questioned about this experience, they all recount what a phenomenal rate of climb the diminutive fighter had.

Following the 27th FEW's run of aerial success early in the New Year, F-84 kills had been thin on the ground. In fact, only a single aircraft had been credited to the Thunderjet since 1Lt Kratt had 'bagged' his Yak-3 on 26 January – 182nd FBS pilots 1 Lt Arthur E Oligher and Capt Harry L Underwood had shared a MiG-15 on 26 June. This was all about to change.

On 19 September a solitary MiG dropped down through an overcast sky right in front of a formation of 49th FBW aircraft. The 9th FBS's Executive Officer, Capt Kenneth L Skeen, reacted the quickest, claiming the 49th FBW's first aerial victory over Korea. He recalls the details of that mission;

'On the 19th, the group was briefed for a dive-bombing mission on the MSR. It was a rail line between Sinanju and Pyongyang. The mission objective was to continue the daily rail cutting at a "choke point" just south of Sukchon where the line crossed a marshy area

between two small hills. This made it very difficult to repair any damage. It was a maximum effort, with all three squadrons putting up 16 aircraft each. That would give us 96 500-lb bombs to do the job with. It was the 9th's second mission of the day, and only my third in the F-84.

'Since inexperience has no rank, I was flying the No 4 slot in the last flight, using the call sign of "Purple Four". After crossing the bomb line north of Seoul, we began flying over broken clouds, which thickened to a heavy overcast as we passed east of Pyongyang.

'Minutes later, we heard the group leader call "MiGs at seven o'clock high". I assumed the F-86s would take care of them as they had on my first two missions. Later on, we found out that our top cover had never gotten airborne – we were on our own. For the past few days, all three squadrons had encountered some resistance from the MiGs, especially when this far north, and there was a lot of radio chatter, mostly about the enemy fighters. When I heard the order to salvo bombs, I knew we were in trouble. Seconds later, I heard "break right Purple Flight!" I was just hanging on as we went to full throttle. The MiGs overshot their attacking turn and pulled up high to our left as "Purple leader" reversed the turn hard to the left into the attackers.

BELOW A flight of F-84Es from the 159th FBS are caught 'on the wing' during a practice mission over Japan in late 1951. At this stage in the war the squadron was still based at Misawa, and only flying periodic combat missions. Having completed a sortie over North Korea, pilots from this unit would land at Taegu, where their jets were rearmed and refuelled, before they returned north once again to perform a second strike mission. Only after the latter had been completed would they return to Japan (Robert Mason)

'Since I was on the outside of the turn, I started falling behind. As I cut across to the inside of the turn to catch up with my element leader (Maj James Sprinkle), who was way out in front of me, a blue MiG-15 locked onto the major's tail. The pilot apparently never saw me. He was accelerating to get lined up on his quarry, and I was at full throttle trying to line him up. I had him in my gunsight and I took my feet off the rudder pedals to make sure the ship was firing true.

'After one long burst, pieces started flying off the MiG, accompanied by a lot of smoke and flames. As he decelerated, I saw that he was on fire, and pulled up to his left to prevent a mid-air collision.

'At that instant, I saw another blue MiG on the tail of an F-84 and I yelled out "Break-break. MiG on your tail – break right!" I was hoping he would bring the bogey right in front of me. Instead, the enemy pilot pulled up high to the left. As I glanced back to my right, I saw a parachute descending and not an aircraft in sight. I headed back to K-2, as I was below bingo fuel. This was the group's first MiG kill, and needless to say there was a party thrown that night! However, the MiGs had scored a bigger victory in that they had made us jettison our bombs so we were unable to hit our targets.'

The final kill figures that would be published after the war would be heavily slanted in favour of the USAF, and especially the F-86 Sabre. The F-84 would hold its own in these statistics too, despite it not being the aircraft's job to go after the MiGs. If the high altitude enemy fighters came down to where the Thunderjets were operating, then the performance advantage of the MiG-15 at altitude became less of a factor. During the course of the war, countless numbers of communist jet pilots would overshoot their targets at medium to low altitudes and end up getting 'hosed' by the F-84s before they could scramble back up onto their 'perch'.

ABOVE *Next to napalm, Thunderjet pilots rated the F-84's six nose-mounted 0.5-in Colt-Browning M3 machine guns as the jet's deadliest weapon. They were usually 'fired out' on every mission, meaning that the armourers back at base were kept busy on the bore sight range. This photograph was taken from the cockpit of 182nd FBS Thunderjet FS-386 whilst its guns were being sighted and their convergence angles accurately set (Wayne Jenkins)*

This panoramic view of Taegu AB, taken on a clear day from a hill above the base, shows long rows of F-84s belonging to the 49th and 136th FBGs. At any given time from mid-1951 through to war's end, there were close to 100 of these fighter-bombers on base. Both groups specialised in the interdiction role, and their exploits north of the 38th Parallel were legendary (Bill Boland)

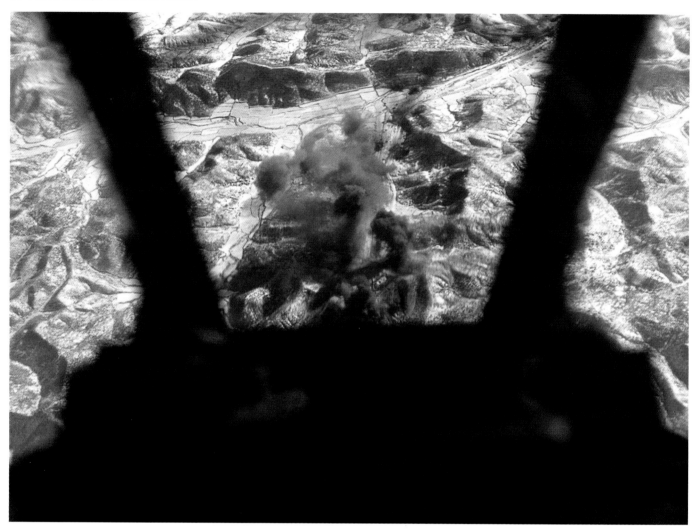

ABOVE *This is the view of the target enjoyed by 182nd FBS Thunderjet pilot Lt Hatold Beasley as he dived on a suspected Chinese troop concentration along the MSR. The aircraft in front of Lt Beasley had already hit the target prior to him starting his bomb run. This unique photograph was taken during the winter of 1951-52 (Harold Beasley)*

The 8th FBS's 1Lt William L Skliar recounts one such engagement that resulted in him claiming a confirmed 'probable';

'My MiG-15 "probable" was originally credited as a "damaged" claim, but after some review boards went over it, it was upgraded. Anyhow, I was leading a four-ship on a rail cutting mission which was part of Operation *Strangle*. We had successfully dive-bombed our targets and were pulling out when we got jumped by several MiGs.

'There were quite a few of them, and I called out a break into the lead MiG – when he saw us turn into him, he reversed his turn. Another one then came across, turning about 1200 ft in front of us, its engine running at maximum power. I laid my F-84 into as tight a turn as possible and managed to draw a lead. We were at maximum range for our 0.50-cals, but I got some good long bursts in.

'Then I glanced over my shoulder to see where the other ones were, and when I looked forward again, my MiG was nowhere in sight. We were already aware that they often tried to decoy us into chasing them so the other ones could get on our tails. This decoy, however, came a bit too close for his own good. My gun camera film showed fuel streaming from the wing root areas on both sides. It was doubtful that he was able to make it back across the river, and to the best of our knowledge there were no suitable landing areas around there, so he must have gone in.'

By the autumn of 1951, the 116th FBW had settled into its rather boring routine of flying the Northern Area Defense Alert over Japan. All three squadrons were anxious to get into the war, and it was the Chitose-based 196th that would be the first to experience combat, followed by the 158th. Flying from the main F-84 base at Taegu, the latter unit accomplished the following achievements during its solitary week in action in December 1951 – 12 rail cuts, 23 buildings destroyed and one MiG-15 shot down (by Capt Paul C Mitchell) and a further three damaged.

LEFT *The famous Indian's head emblem of the 154th FBS adorned the unit's Operations building at Taegu AB in 1951. Prior to being activated for the Korean War, the unit served with the Arkansas ANG, flying F-51D Mustangs from Adams Field in Little Rock (Bill Ahring)*

OPERATION *STRANGLE*

Once UN Intelligence learned just how many Chinese troops were fighting in Korea, they passed this information onto the FEAF. A master plan was devised that would hamper the Chinese logistics efforts to the extent that they would not be able to mount any serious offensive. Known as Operation *Strangle*, it accomplished more than could have ever been imagined. The F-84 was to be a key player in this operation, and that was the primary reason why more Thunderjets where allocated to the FEAF during the early summer of 1951.

In theory, the increased range of the Republic fighter-bomber would allow those wings equipped with the jet to intercept and destroy all Chinese military supplies at source, rather than in the frontline. The bulk of the *Strangle* missions would be aimed at the Yalu River and the main supply routes that ran deep in the northern sectors of Korea.

By the end of December 1951, the F-84 squadrons in-theatre had flown over 30,000 combat sorties, which equated to 65,000 hours of flying time. This was a phenomenal record, although one must remember that other fighter-bomber types were also performing their share of missions too – F-80s and F-51s were flying close support sorties over the frontline, and night-marauding B-26s were keeping the pressure on the enemy during the hours of darkness. Land-based Marine Corps units were also heavily involved, as were US Navy and Royal Navy squadrons flying from carriers off the coast.

Operation *Strangle* was probably the largest single aerial undertaking of the war. Devised by World War 2 B-24 veteran and now Fifth Air Force Commander, Maj-Gen Edward J Timberlake, its aim was to completely shut off the movement of supplies along the three main road/rail routes that connected the 39th Parallel with the frontline. To achieve this, single routes were allocated to

BELOW A 9th FBS F-84E is seen during a brief visit to Kimpo AB (K-14) in the early autumn of 1951, the unit's red and white chevron marking being clearly visible on the jet's tail (Earl Plesia)

the Fifth Air Force, 1st Marine Air Wing and the navy's Task Force 77. All three organisations committed every available asset to *Strangle*, inflicting unparalleled levels of destruction on Chinese military forces in their respective areas. The operation officially began on 31 May 1951, despite the main F-84 force having not yet settled in. Missions would be flown around the clock, with no let-up unless the weather intervened.

By September, the demands of this operation forced the 136th FBG to move from Itazuke to Taegu, which in turn meant that the group's trio of squadrons could fly many more sorties, and thus increase their effectiveness. The group's relocation to Korea coincided with an upsurge in MiG activity, as the Chinese attempted to reopen their bombed-out supply routes. Fighter-bomber pilots could now expect to encounter communist fighters on just about every mission that ventured north of Pyongyang. The large number of MiGs coming south of the river did have an effect on *Strangle* sorties, for many flights had to salvo their ordnance prematurely because they had been jumped before they could complete their bombing runs.

The three squadrons of the 136th found themselves particularly busy flying dangerous missions up along the Yalu River during the October/November period. Although these sorties were all a part of the now long-running Operation *Strangle*, the targets they were being allocated had become better defended, with swarms of MiG-15s overhead and mobile flak batteries accompanying all train and truck convoys.

ABOVE *Lt Quinn Fuller (in his 'poopy suit') of the 8th FBS steps into the cockpit of* THE ROUNDER *at the start of a long-range bombing mission to the north-eastern corner of Korea. This photograph was taken in early January 1952 at the height of a bitterly cold Korean winter. Nicknamed the 'Black Sheep', the 8th adorned its aircraft with yellow and black tail fin chevrons, yellow tip tank arrows, a yellow intake ring and all-yellow nose gear doors. Note that Quinn Fuller also has a yellow and black striped helmet, which has been sat on the wing until he has completed the strapping in process. Two 1000-lb GP bombs have been fitted to the wing pylons of the jet (Quinn Fuller)*

Despite the improved defence of targets, the seemingly constant cycle of sorties continued. In October, the 154th FBS alone flew 617 sorties and made 238 rail cuts (equating to over 300 tons of ordnance dropped), which it followed up in November with a further 555 flights. Astoundingly, the 154th suffered only three air and nine ground aborts during the latter month. The squadron records for both the 111th and 182nd reveal similar statistics, and at Taegu the 49th FBG was flying a near-identical number of sorties.

AMAZING ESCAPE

In any war, there are always amazing stories of bravery and extraordinary feats. Some surface through press coverage at the time, whilst others remain untold. On 16 December 1951, one of the most dramatic, and widely publicised, incidents of the Korean air war occurred during a mission involving F-84s from the 154th FBS.

Capt John L Paladino was leading his flight of four Thunderjets on a routine mission to cut a specific stretch of railway track. The pilots all dropped their bombs successfully through light flak, and had commenced the return flight to Taegu when, at 32,000 ft Capt Paladino's oxygen equipment malfunctioned. He slipped into a state of unconsciousness, but fortunately for him, his plight was spotted by Capt Jack Miller and Lt Wood Arthur. The former pilot recalls the incident;

'We were headed south at high altitude when all of a sudden John's aircraft started to turn, and then went into a steep dive to the left. I thought that he was maybe prac-

LEFT *Personnel from the 116th FBW had come from the warm climates of California and Florida, where winter weather meant temperatures in the 'mid-sixties'. This left them ill-prepared for the bitter Japanese winter, which lasted for around five months. Here, armourers attempt to load belts of 0.5-in ammunition into the breeches of a 159th FBS F-84E at Misawa AB in late 1951, their frozen fingers making this job almost impossible to complete. Note the refuelling probe grafted onto the starboard tip tank of the aircraft closest to the camera (Robert Mason)*

FAR LEFT *This elevated view, taken from the control tower at Misawa, shows a pair of 'defrosted' F-84Es from the 158th FBS being readied for flight. Part of the 116th FBW, the unit was still involved in the Air Defense role for the area when this photograph was taken in late 1951. However, all three squadrons controlled by the wing were also conducting periodic 'Skat' missions over North Korea at the same time (Robert Mason)*

MAIN PICTURE *Thunderjets based in Korea regularly used JATO bottles when taking off with a full load of ordnance and fuel, particularly during the warm summer months. Side-by-side take-offs were also common practice within most F-84 units operating on Korean soil. Each loaded with a pair of 500-lb GP bombs, two 7th FBS jets are seen nearing the point of rotation at Taegu in the autumn of 1951 (Richard Immig)*

INSET *The maintenance crews from the 49th FBG strove to ensure that the jets 'in-service' level amongst its trio of units was always above the air force's norm for the Thunderjet. These neatly-parked 8th FBS F-84Es are being readied for their next mission from Taegu, the groundcrews working out of the maintenance huts situated to the right of the flightline. Everything that was needed to keep the aircraft airworthy was located within close proximity of the stationary fighter-bombers (Lynn Balow)*

tising evasive action or something. After he had gone down several thousand feet, his plane did a "pitch-up", which was characteristic of the Thunderjet when it went through the speed of sound. After a couple of simple dives and sudden climbs, he was still on course, so we figured he was okay.

'When I pulled up alongside his aircraft, I noticed that he was tugging at his oxygen mask. He said he was all right, so I told him to throttle back for the descent home. As we inched closer, I noticed that John's head was resting against the canopy. Before I could call him, he slumped forward. At that time I knew what the problem was, and that we had to get him down to an altitude that would bring him back around. Without hesitation, I told Lt Arthur to put one of his wings under one of John's and I would do the same on my side. The flow of air over the wingtips would keep his aircraft straight and level without our wings touching his. We remained in this close formation for about 100 miles (15 minutes).

'We inched him down to about 15,000 ft, and at that time he began to nod his head a little. About 2000 ft lower, he snapped into a very alert state, and was capable of landing his aircraft at Taegu on his own!'

Upon climbing out of the cockpit, Paladino complained of a violent headache, which was far better than the alternative. This act of heroism was reported in most newspapers and *Life* magazine. All three pilots safely finished their 100 missions and returned back to their homes in Arkansas.

Pilots from the 154th FBS received further accolades on 8 January 1952, when the unit became the first to fire an 11.75-in 'Tiny Tim' rocket from an F-84. This event was greeted with relief by the squadron's long-suffering groundcrews, who had expended much effort 'in the field' solving the problem of attaching the 550-lb semi-armour piercing warhead to the 750-lb rocket motor. Hardly a precision-guided munition, the accuracy of 'Tiny Tim' left a lot to be desired, but if it did manage to hit what it was aimed at, you would be assured of complete destruction of the target! The first known use of the rocket by a USAF aircraft in Korea was by the 35th FBS, which fired several rounds from its F-51 Mustangs in the autumn of 1950. 'Acquired' from a nearby Marine squadron, these early rockets achieved less than encouraging results.

With the arrival of more MiG-15s in late 1951, new tactics were employed by the communist pilots against the fighter-bombers. These had originally been devised in an effort to reduce the losses suffered against F-86s, and were witnessed up close by Thunderjet pilot Lt Donald R James of the 8th FBS;

BELOW Soon after the 159th FBS arrived in Japan from George AFB, in California, it commenced an intensive training programme to strengthen its skills in the Air Defense mission. This was the squadron's primary role whilst attached to the FEAF, and although the unit would periodically fly combat missions over Korea, it would never permanently operate from a base in-theatre (Robert Mason)

'On 23 November 1951 I was on my 28th combat mission over North Korea. Thirty-seven F-84s from the 49th FBG took off from Taegu and headed for railroad tracks at Sukchon, some 150 miles north of the 39th Parallel. I was in the No 2 slot. As we arrived in the target area, radio chatter informed us that enemy fighters had already taken off from Antung.

'All went well as we put our bombs on the tracks in trail. We came off our run and turned west, heading for the Yellow Sea. We stayed right on the deck and fire-walled the throttle, pushing the speed up to the limits. As we cleared the target area I would always look for the F-84 ahead of me, joining up over the water in an effort to provide each other with mutual protection. On this day, the MiGs suddenly appeared all over the sky, and most were down at our level – somehow, they had evaded the Sabres. They were using weird tactics against us, diving down from about 5000 ft in trail with each other, speed brakes out and making 90-degree angle passes at us.

'For some reason or another, the MiGs had not learned a hard fact yet! The F-84 without its ordnance load, and on internal fuel and going very fast below 15,000 ft, is a better fighter than the MiG-15 – hands

ABOVE *Flying over North Korean mountains, these 9th FBS Thunderjets are seen heading south during the return leg of a long-range bombing mission. This photograph was taken in September 1951 when Operation Strangle was in full swing, and both Korean-based F-84 groups were performing a staggering number of sorties per day in support of it. Aside from attacking countless ground targets during this phase of the operation, the 9th FBS also scored its first MiG-15 kill (Charles Willis)*

down! One enemy fighter made a 90-degree pass at the F-84 directly in front of Lt Shellem, missed and kept right on going across our flightpath without turning. Shellem, at this time, was much faster than the MiG, and he turned right into him in a perfect gunnery pass.

'Whilst performing this manoeuvre, Shellem became the target for a second MiG, which came barrelling through the formation and tried to tack onto his F-84. I was in an excellent position to turn into the second one, and we were starting a "daisy chain" at zero altitude and going "balls out"! Shellem started to fire about the time the first MiG pilot woke up, retracted his speed brakes and throttled up.

'The No 2 MiG caught on at the same time, and his speed brakes came in and he accelerated out of our formation at a phenomenal rate. He forgot about continuing his pass on Shellem. I fired a lengthy burst at the second MiG from long range, in spite of the fact that I still had my gunsight in the dive-bomb mode, and the pipper was depressed 20 degrees, making it useless for air-to-air gunnery. Shellem, however, remained cool, hosing his MiG down with some accurate rounds. He was later given credit for "damaging" his target in the encounter. On later missions, we were attacked numerous times, but they never used these tactics again!'

BELOW 'Iron Knights' from the 9th FBS pose at Taegu in late 1951. All had flown myriad combat missions in both F-80Cs and F-84Es by the time this group shot was taken. Amongst this clutch of aviators are Capt Arnold Braswell (fourth from the right), who would later achieve the rank of lieutenant-general before retiring, and Capt Kenneth Skeen (second from the right), who scored the 49th FBG's first MiG-15 kill (Arnold Braswell)

OPERATION *STRANGLE* – F-84 STATISTICS*
(July-December 1951)

Target	136th FBG	49th FBG	Total
Rail Cuts	2335	1779	4114
Buildings	1943	1880	3823
Vehicles	216	203	419
Bridges	88	39	127
Railroad tunnels	18	4	22
Locomotives	31	56	87
Railroad Cars	1343	688	2031
Supply Carts	76	33	109
Boats	89	3	92
Tanks	6	2	8
Gun Positions	126	0	126
Supply Dumps	19	14	33
Highway Cuts	18	18	36
Artillery Pieces	30	96	126
Troop Casualties	578	432	1010

Source – Fifth Air Force Records (FEAF)

CHAPTER THREE

INTERDICTION ROLE INTENSIFIES

By early 1952, the continual pressure exerted by Operation *Strangle* on both Chinese troops in the frontline and their main supply routes had worn the communists down to such a degree that it was now proving difficult for them to mount any type of serious offensive. Indeed, the campaign had been so effective that by early March the number of targets that were left 'up north' had dwindled to the point where F-84s were now available to flying close air support missions over the frontline as well.

On 26 March both the 136th and 49th FBGs began working directly with UN troops. For pilots used to travelling hundreds of miles into enemy territory, operating with forward air controllers (FACs) who rarely ventured beyond visual distance of the frontline took some getting used to. Figures for April show that both groups devoted

five days out of the month to performing the close support mission, with the remainder of their sorties being flown against 'traditional' targets such as railway lines and truck routes situated throughout North Korea.

Although the threat of an immediate offensive had been negated, UN intelligence continued to search for evidence of a major build-up of supplies north of the frontline. When such a stockpile was discovered, it was immediately 'taken out' by at least one squadron of Thunderjets. Such missions had top priority, for the UN realised that the only way to keep the numerically superior communist forces at bay was to starve them of sufficient reserves to sustain any new offensive. This in turn forced the Chinese to scatter their supplies over a large area, preventing them from supporting any push southwards.

BELOW *A perfect day for bombing! These 182nd FBS F-84s are heading deep into North Korea with their bomb loads. This photograph was taken in 1952 by Lt Harold Beasley, flying in the right slot position (Harold Beasley)*

MAIN PICTURE *These colourful 182nd FBS F-84Es are seen forming up for the return flight to Taegu after successfully completing a bombing mission over 'MiG Alley'. The mountainous terrain visible below the jets indicates that they are still some way north of the 38th Parallel. Red trim was carried by aircraft assigned to the 182nd FBS, which was part of the 136th FBG. In peacetime, the squadron had flown F-51Ds from Brooks AFB in San Antonio as part of the Texas ANG (J D Brown)*

INSET *The 136th FBG took over aircraft left behind by the vacating 27th FEW, this particular Thunderjet being assigned to the 154th FBS. Like the 182nd FBS, the 154th had been equipped with F-51Ds when called to active duty in October 1950, serving with the Arkansas ANG at Adams Field in Little Rock. The 136th commenced combat operations on 1 August 1951, and remained in the FEAF until replaced by the 58th FBG in July 1952. 'Bombed up' with 1000-lb GPs, this aircraft was photographed at Taegu AB in the early summer of 1952 (Cale Herry)*

ABOVE *Posted in the heart of the 7th FBS's 'patch' at Taegu, this sign has been hastily modified for the benefit of the camera. The famous nude calendar shot of Marilyn Monroe was undoubtedly the most popular poster pinned up by military personnel in the Far East during the Korean War. Later in the conflict, Ms Monroe actually paid the troops a visit in Korea, this event still being remembered today by those soldiers fortunate enough to see her. She even found time to call in on one of the F-84 units while in-theatre (M F Read)*

Of those targets still deemed worthy of attacking in North Korea, locomotives had to be at the top of the 'most wanted' list for any F-84 pilot. However, with very few now running during daylight hours, it was mostly left to the night attack pilots to claim the bulk of the engines destroyed in 1952. During the day trains would seek shelter in the myriad rail tunnels scattered across North Korea, although F-84 pilots soon became proficient in bombing these mountain hideaways, as Lt Patrick Halloran of the 58th FBW recalls;

'It was a pre-dawn take-off for one of those "first light" recce strikes that we had been involved in for the past month or so. Some very interesting things were observed over North Korea when the sun's rays first began to light up the sky. All nocturnal activities had to be closed down for the day, and unit movements and logistic efforts hidden from view before UN aircraft started looking for targets.

'We had spent months on *Strangle*, cutting rail lines and highways in an effort to reduce the flow of supplies to the front. The results were mixed, as thousands of labourers could fix most of the damage within hours. Trains seldom moved during the daylight, and it was

known that they hid inside the hundreds of rail tunnels, only to resume operations as soon as night fell. Our job with the "first light" reconnaissance missions was to try and find the tunnels which contained the trains and attack their sanctuary using skip-bombing techniques. If everything worked right, a good fighter-bomber pilot could approach a tunnel right on the deck, release his bombs just before reaching its mouth and, through a combination of skill and luck, deliver them right inside to where the trains were hiding.

'I have absolutely no idea as to the actual statistics on our success rate, but I know that a number of deliveries were made right on target by many of our pilots. We ascertained whether the tunnel was "live" or not by the presence of escaping steam coming out of the opening. By getting there right at dawn, we could usually spot such indications before they dissipated. Another thing to look for around a "live" tunnel was a proliferation of "Triple-A" defences, which definitely made it a "hot" area to enter! That was particularly true when you were near the tail end of the attacking formation! Another obvious hazard was that tunnels meant mountains, and manoeuvring your aircraft on the deck, at high speed, heading right at the side of a well-armed mountain, was not a game for the faint of heart!'

HIGH TIDE

In the opening week of 1952, the 116th FBW was selected to work on a new project code-named Operation *High Tide*. The results of this special assignment would help revolutionise the role of air power in combat, for the wing was tasked with perfecting the concept of tactical aerial refuelling. To complete the task, the 116th would be working with ex-SAC Superfortresses that had been modified into KB-29 tankers.

Within 90 days of the commencement of *High Tide*, most of the pilots within the wing had received their aerial refuelling qualification. However, the 158th FBS's conversion had been temporarily interrupted on 21 February, when it was ordered to send all 18 of its Thunderjets to Taegu to fly bombing missions against a major rail junction north-east of Pyongyang. Unfortunately, poor weather over the target meant that the results achieved by the unit's glide-bombing attack could not be confirmed, and it returned to Misawa after just two days in Korea. And with the 158th back in Japan, the routine of *High Tide* sorties returned to normal.

All pilots had become proficient in aerial refuelling by the end of April, and the wing duly declared itself available for action. FEAF HQ had been monitoring the progress of the tests, and in early May rumours began circulating in Japan that *High Tide* might manifest itself in the form of missions into North Korea. Finally, on the 28th of the month 16 aircraft took off from Misawa and flew to Itazuke. Here, pilots received final briefings for a mission against a variety of targets in the North Korean city of Sariwon, south of Pyongyang.

Each F-84 took off loaded with two 500-lb GP bombs, the mission plan calling for each pilot to refuel at altitude over Taegu, before pressing north to bomb the targets and then recovering back at Johnson AB, in Japan. This first mission went so successfully that near-identical strikes were flown on 7 June, 22 June and 4 July, this latter date also coinciding with the the completion of *High Tide*.

HEAVY LOSSES

During the first five months of 1952, the attrition rate amongst F-84 squadrons in the FEAF had been higher than ever before. Many of these losses were due to accelerated sortie rates, combined with a drastic increase in the number of Chinese anti-aircraft guns in-theatre. The

BELOW This replacement 7th FBS F-84 (lacking the unit's distinctive black and white chevrons on the vertical stabiliser) is seen resting on its belly at the end of the runway at Taegu AB after suffering an engine failure on take-off. The standard procedure for pilots to follow should this occur when carrying ordnance was for them to jettison the stores whilst still on the runway, retract the undercarriage and sit tight and enjoy the ride! The snow and icy conditions have helped to reduce the amount of damage inflicted on this particular aircraft, and it was almost certainly repaired and returned to regular mission rotation within days of this photograph being taken (Leonard Guiton)

latter now accompanied all truck convoys, troop movements and supply trains. Such were the losses suffered by the Thunderjet units that by the end of April (one of the worst months for F-84 attrition) the 49th FBG had only 41 operational jets instead of the authorised strength of 90. A decision had to be made quickly as to how these units would be re-stocked, and it was decided that 102 older D-models would have to be pulled from units in the USA and sent to Korea.

With a large number of F-84Es already in-theatre, the FEAF now faced a potential maintenance nightmare as units would have to attempt to operate two differently-engined models of Thunderjet side-by-side. However, prior to any F-84Ds arriving in Korea, it was decided that they should all be assigned to the 136th FBG, who would in turn transfer its surviving F-84Es to the chronically understrength 49th FBG. The respective conversions were completed in late May.

Following the infusion of E-model Thunderjets, the latter group immediately renewed its bombing efforts along the Yalu River, where rail interdiction missions were proving extremely hazardous due to the close proximity of the MiG base at Antung. One such mission occurred on 6 June, as Lt W J Heath relates;

'We were going after a stretch of tracks up around Chong-ju, near the river. We knew there would be MiGs in the area, but we concentrated on our objective. We lined up in single file and went in just a few seconds apart. When we were pulling up after bomb release, three MiG-15s jumped us. Before I knew it, one of them was locked on my tail, and there were orange golf balls all around my aircraft. Even with violent evasive action, he got several hits on me, although his attack didn't last long, as I believe he shot off all of his ammunition.

'I finally got up to altitude and headed back to base, experiencing no apparent problems in controlling the ship. But when I landed and did a walk-around check on my jet, I counted 80 holes in my F-84, including one through the right wing that measured over 18 inches in diameter – this was almost certainly caused by a single 37 mm cannon round. There was so much damage to the right landing gear strut that my groundcrew was hesitant about even

BELOW This view illustrates why the Thunderjet was the USAF's natural choice for the air-to-ground mission – the aircraft's ability to fly long distances armed with two 1000-lb GP bombs, 0.5-in machine guns and four 5-in HVARs (High Velocity Aircraft Rockets). In addition to this 'mix' of ordnance, the F-84 was capable of absorbing multiple hits during the course of a mission and still make it safely back to base. This particular aircraft was assigned to the 7th FBS (John Glanton)

towing the fighter back to the squadron dispersal. Republic sure had built one tough aeroplane!'

Four days prior to Lt Heath's memorable sortie (flown on 2 June 1952), 7th FBS pilot Lt Leonard A Guiton had also encountered MiGs during a squadron-strength mission to temporarily shut down the rail links that connected Chong-ju with the frontline. Flying in the number two slot, he remembers;

'We proceeded to the IP and went into elements in trail formation as we set up for our bomb runs. Bandits had earlier been sighted in the area, and my flight was briefed to hold element integrity. We entered our bomb runs at approximately 8000 ft, lined up the rails and dropped. One of my bombs was observed hitting dead centre, taking a section out.

'We broke off of the target and climbed to between 4000 and 6000 ft, using flak evasion tactics on the way to our rendezvous out over the water. At this moment we were bounced by four MiG-15s that were barrelling in on our number three man from his five o'clock position.

'We waited until they were within firing range and then broke hard right – a little too late for our number three, as he radioed that he had been hit in the right wing. As I was halfway through my break, I observed a dull grey MiG-15 in front of me and slightly low. He was at my

two o'clock and pulling up in front of me. I got my pipper lined up and began to track him. I fired about 130 rounds out of each of my six machine guns, and I observed light smoke coming from the MiG as it climbed steadily away from me. I broke off and joined up with my element leader, and we headed back to Taegu.

'We could expect this type of interference on just about any mission we flew up close to the river. At least there were very few surprises!'

KEY TARGETS

During the first week of June 1952, UN mission planners had determined that it was time to tackle the most significant series of targets left intact in North Korea – the massive hydro-electric plants located at Suiho, Fusen, Choshin and Kyosen. Up until this time, they had been off limits for countless reasons, but now they had been deemed legitimate targets. F-84s from the 49th and 136th FBGs would be involved in destroying the plants, supplying as many aircraft as they could to the mission. Also included in this operation would be F-51s and F-80s from the 8th and 18th FBWs respectively.

The master plan called for all four power complexes to be hit simultaneously, which meant that aircraft from both the marines and the navy would also be involved.

ABOVE *Itazuke AB in Japan was the major maintenance centre for all F-84s in-theatre, and most of the aircraft seen here undergoing servicing wear the markings of the 49th FBG's 7th FBS. Note that replacement aircraft FS-655-B (in the middle left of the photograph) still wears the red markings of its previous squadron, based in the USA (Frederic Champlin)*

Combined Task Force 77 would launch 230 aircraft from the carriers *Boxer, Princeton, Philippine Sea* and *Bon Homme Richard*, which would join the 270-strong USAF fighter-bomber force and various attack aircraft from Marine Air Groups' 12 and 33. Finally, patrolling above this impressive force would be over 100 Sabres from the 4th and 51st FIWs. However, their job was not to watch what was going on below them, but instead to monitor the activities of the MiG-15 bases north of the Yalu. This would be the first large-scale air operation of the Korean War to make use of aircraft from all the various US air elements in-theatre.

The attack began at exactly 1601 hours on 23 June 1952. Intelligence sources were uncertain as to how well-defended these targets would be, since they had received very little attention up until this time. Therefore, the first aircraft to attack the plants were several flights of dedicated flak suppression navy F9F Panthers, whose initial strafing runs were followed by a large number of navy Skyraiders and all available Thunderjets. Each of the fighter-bombers were carrying their maximum loads, and their 1000-lb bombs did irreparable damage to many key areas within the plants.

The most surprising aspect of the attack was that the strike on the Suiho complex, which was within sight of the MiG base at Antung, provoked little response from the nearby communist fighters. Visual counts by F-86 pilots placed at least 210 MiGs lined up on the ramp at Antung, and during the brief duration of the main attack, several enemy fighters took off and headed north into Manchuria.

Quite what happened at Antung that day has been the source of much speculation ever since. Certain informed observers have stated that either the base commander thought the large number of attack aircraft in the vicinity were meant for his base, or that those pilots that did take off were frightened by the superior number of fighters overhead, making them fly north instead of south. Whatever the cause, the lack of aggressive action by the MiG-15s resulted in all of the targets being left without any form of serious protection.

Within two hours of the attack beginning, a significant percentage of North Korea's power production had been temporarily shut down. The key to inflicting permanent damage to these generators was in the execution of follow-up attacks flown on an almost daily basis over the coming week. Due to the employment of a complicated

BELOW *This 9th FBS Thunderjet has been loaded with two 500-lb GP bombs in preparation for an interdiction mission against a target north of Pyongyang. By the autumn of 1952, UN air attacks against the main rail lines between Manchuria and Pyongyang had become so effective that large numbers of MiG-15s were encountered far south of their normal territory attempting to intercept flights of bomb-laden F-84s (Robert Bunten)*

LEFT *Taken in late 1952, this photograph graphically shows just how much groundfire F-84 pilots faced when at the bottom of their dive-bombing runs over a target. Chinese troops would usually fire their guns at random into the air whenever a jet was seen overhead, thus throwing up a wall of bullets that was often difficult to evade. Riddled with holes, the yellow and black chevrons on the vertical stabiliser of this F-84 denote its assignment to the 8th FBS at Taegu (Charles Scofield)*

The packed flightline at Kunsan (K-8). The yellow-tailed Thunderjets were from the 430th FBS/474th FBG, whilst the B-26s in the background belonged to the 3rd Bomb Group. Sandwiched between the USAF types is a visiting F2H-2P Banshee tactical reconnaissance aircraft from the Marine Corps' VMJ-1. The 'flying leathernecks' maintained a permanent presence at Kunsan in the form of nightfighter squadron VMF(N)-513, and its all-black F3D Skynights (Ed Galbraith)

RIGHT *An unidentified 7th FBS pilot runs through his preflight checklist with his crew chief as he prepares for his next mission. Below the 'star and bar' are two JATO bottles, which became a mandatory fixture on heavily-laden F-84s at Taegu during the hot summer months in Korea. The external 'weapons of the day' on this particular aircraft are a pair of 1000-lb GP bombs. Note that even as late as 1952, the ramp at Taegu was still unpaved (Lynn Balow)*

BOTTOM RIGHT *One of the best photos to be taken over North Korea. The pilot in the left slot Thunderjet is leading the rest of his flight to targets beyond the North Korean capital, which is just visible at the top left hand corner of the photograph. The red chevrons on the aircraft's tail denote its assignment to the 9th FBS (nicknamed the 'Iron Knights'). Note the ice and snow that has blanketed the mountainous terrain below. This shot was taken in late 1952 (Ed Galbraith)*

OPPOSITE *An armourer from the 49th FBG's 7th FBS makes adjustments to the feeding mechanism on one of the 0.5-in guns fitted to this aircraft. Every F-84 in the group was worked hard to fulfil the FEAF's tasking requirements against road and rail traffic that plied the main supply routes between Manchuria and the frontline (F I Stone)*

interlocking power grid system in North Korea, if one generator was working, the electricity it produced could be 'shunted off' in several directions to help take up the 'slack' caused by generators that had been knocked out.

And within days of the first attack, UN intelligence picked up reports that a large number of Russian and Chinese technicians had been rushed in to help get the damaged elements working again.

The F-84s and Skyraiders had been the 'heavy haulers' during the attacks on the power stations, carrying the most destructive power within the strike package. For the remainder of 1952, and continuing on into the spring of 1953, all of these hydro-electric plants ranked highly on the priority target list for the fighter-bomber squadrons. Virtually every F-84 pilot in-theatre during this period flew numerous missions against these targets during the course of their respective tours.

474th FBW

In July 1952 the 116th FBW completed its spell with the the FEAF and was replaced by the 474th FBW, who in turn took over the wing's battle-weary Thunderjets. Simultaneously, the decision was made that all F-84 units would from then on operate from Korean soil, eliminating the Air Defence of Japan role carried out by the 116th during its time in-theatre. The 474th immediately moved up to Kunsan (K-8), and commenced combat operations.

This base change put three full groups of Thunderjets in Korea, and for the next 12 months they would face a determined Chinese logistics effort attempting to support a planned new offensive aimed at driving UN ground forces far south of the 38th Parallel.

After a full year of combat operations, the 136th FBW was also rotated back to the United States in mid-1952. In its place came the newly-activated 58th FBW, which had been formed at Itazuke AB just prior to the 136th officially ending its active military service in Korea at 2400 hours on 9 July. None of the numerous changeovers that were experienced by F-84 units during the war ever disrupted combat operations.

The 58th FBW's trio of squadrons – the 69th, 310th and 311th FBSs – wasted no time in setting a torrid pace of bombing missions over enemy territory. Less than 30 days after getting its 'feet wet' in action, the wing participated in one of the biggest raids of the war against heavily defended targets in the North Korean capital of Pyongyang. The three squadrons flew 101 sorties on a single day without suffering the loss of a single Thunderjet!

Lt Roy Pitsch served with the 69th FBS during 1952-53, and he participated in several of the hazardous close support and deep interdiction missions that the 58th FBW flew during his time in the frontline. His comments reflect the strategies that pilots used to survive;

'Most of our work was done at low altitude, which meant that the biggest threat we faced was from the hail of small arms fire emanating from enemy troops on the ground. We lost a lot of good pilots due to them getting "hosed" at the bottom of their bomb runs. Once, I took a hit in the right wing fuel pump, but the tank was empty so there was no fire or loss of control.

'One of the tricks we used – especially around the Pyongyang area, which was heavily defended with radar controlled guns – was to come in at a high altitude to avoid the flak, make our bomb runs and then race out to sea following the river at the lowest altitude that we felt safe at. This forced the enemy gunners to hold their fire on both sides of the river or risk shooting each other. We

reassembled over the ocean out of their range and then headed back to Taegu.

'I can remember another mission where we were to bomb a supply dump located in a narrow valley. Once again, we had a problem with scattered cloud cover, and the flight leader elected to approach the target in a crosswise direction to the valley. He did this in order to get a better shot at the target. All went well until I attempted to release my bombs – they did not let go! Normally, your pull-out of the dive is calculated on losing the weight of the bomb load. This time I still had the bombs attached, and a mountain was covering my windscreen.

'There was a shallow "saddle" in the crest of the mountain so I headed for it, pulling back on the stick as hard as I could without inducing a high speed stall, which would have mushed me right into the side of the mountain! The "saddle" sank below me as I saw tree-tops passing by. I went back up to 8000 ft, toggled the arming switch and attempted to drop the bombs from there. This time they released.

'After I got back to base, I inspected the wingtips and found green stains and fragments of tree-top stuck in the panel seams around the navigation lights. I went back into the operations shack, where we had fresh coffee and a bar. I found a bottle of bourbon and poured myself a large

BELOW *This photograph of a 9th FBS Thunderjet was taken from an elevated workstand next to the flightline at K-2. Whilst the pilot prepares to don his helmet, his crew chief gives the canopy a final check, prior to pulling it shut. The fighter-bomber is equipped with two 1000-lb GP bombs (Ed Galbraith)*

RIGHT *Lt Harold Beasley of the 182nd FBS snapped this circa 1952 photograph of a direct hit on a suspected enemy troop concentration located on the North Korean coastline. The explosions were the result of ordnance dropped by preceding members of his flight, for Beasley was the last to attack the target (Harold Beasley)*

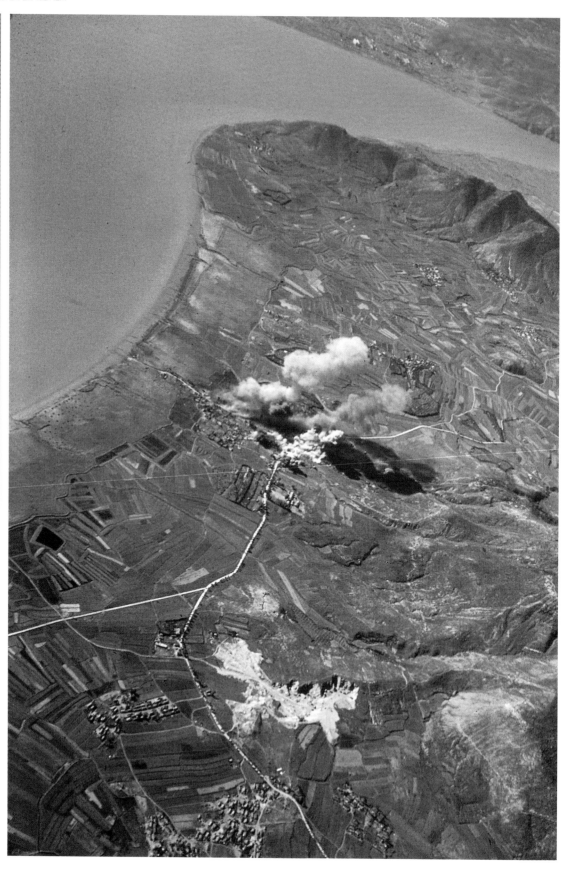

glass to calm my nerves. It was one of the closest calls that I had over there!'

With fewer targets to be found during daylight hours, favourite 'pass-times' such as 'truck hunting' were rapidly becoming little more than a memory for most F-84 pilots. Only night-marauding B-26 Invaders and a handful of Marine nightfighters were now scoring heavily against vehicles running the roads at night. However, despite impressive tallies, their efforts were simply not enough, for North Korea had so many roads (particularly in mountainous areas) that plenty of trucks were still getting through to the frontline. In an effort to remedy this worsening situation, the FEAF ordered a select few F-84 pilots to begin working up in preparation for night intruder missions that would take them into 'MiG Alley'.

Lt Ralph Ritteman, an experienced F-84 pilot in the 474th FG, explains his views on this concept;

'Contention raged as to the effectiveness of these night intruder operations, some claiming that they achieved very little, and others that they worked very well. You can count me in the latter camp. Consider this – of those few of us who had the opportunity to prepare properly and to practice sufficiently to develop some level of confidence in the techniques required, and most of all to go up north the first dozen times or more, then I can tell you that one night intruder mission was worth a lot of day missions! Why? Because in the daytime you seldom saw a truck or train, but at night you could look down at hundreds of them all on the move!

'The amount of destruction you could accomplish was only limited by your ability to dive-bomb and strafe at night. Admittedly, these skills were not acquired in one or two, or even half a dozen, missions. However, once learnt they had a devastating result on the enemy!

'On the subject of trucks, I wondered throughout the war why almost all trucks that took a concentrated burst of 0.5-in Armour-Piercing Incendiary (API) blew up with the same uniform white explosion? After the war was over, I found out the answer to the question – just like western Texas on a Sunday night, it was a long way between gas stations! Each truck carried at least one 50-gallon drum of gas, which produced a standard white explosion. The exceptions to this were the trucks that were loaded with ammunition. They usually blew up with a different, but more spectacular, explosion. We saw plenty of secondary explosions on those night missions.

'One thought that always amused me related to the almost total ineffectiveness of the standard blackout lights with which all military trucks were equipped. The simple truth was that the level of lighting required by a driver to enable him to follow a road at night was also more than enough to render his truck visible to aircraft overhead.'

RAIL CUT REPAIRS

Matching the persistence of the truck drivers were the many repair crews that continually mended the various cuts inflicted on the the railway lines which criss-crossed North Korea. In a matter of hours, hundreds of workers

BELOW The armourers have finished loading 500-lb bombs onto these 111th FBS Thunderjets at Taegu. Note the rocks and dirt surrounding the dispersal at the base, the PSP being the only thing that stopped aircraft from sinking into the mud that became synonymous with the rainy season in Korea (Cale Herry)

These seven F-84 pilots were seasoned 'practitioners' of the 'art' of close air support and interdiction. All were members of the 9th FBS, with the individual on the far right (squatting) being Capt Arnold Braswell. He would go on to enjoy a long and successful career in the USAF, retiring with the rank of lieutenant-general (Arnold Braswell)

ABOVE *One of the more colourfully-painted F-84s in-theatre was the CO's aircraft for the 58th FBW. Decorated with coloured chevrons representing all three units within the wing, as well as fuselage art and various womens' names, the jet is seen here at Taegu flanked by a refuelling cart, a well-worn tractor and an auxiliary power cart. The 58th FBW replaced the 136th FBW on 10 July 1952 (Bill Boland)*

could fix major rail cuts, allowing the trains to run again long before first light. Due to the effectiveness of the interdiction campaign that had been conducted since late 1951, the Chinese moved thousands of labourers into North Korea and stationed them along the stretches of track deemed to be the most vulnerable to UN attacks. Due to the skill and hard work of these teams, fighter-bombers had to repeat these rail cutting missions day after day.

It was finally decided that the only way to deal with this repair effort was to strike while teams were in the process of fixing the rail cuts. Up until 1952 this mission had been handled by a small force of nightflying B-26s, but due to their paucity in number, they found it difficult to deal with the many repair teams in action across North Korea. In an attempt to solve the problem, F-84s flown by night-trained pilots like Lt Milton Riggs (of the 69th FBS) were temporarily assigned to assist the B-26s;

'Due to the huge labour force fielded by the Chinese, they were able to repair any damage we caused to rails, bridges and roads during the day. This was a key factor in bringing the F-84 into the night intruder role. The plan called for a single aircraft to fly into a specified target area, followed by another one 15 minutes later. Each of these

Thunderjets would be armed with two 1000-lb bombs that had proximity fuses timed to explode about 100 ft above the ground. This played havoc with the repair crews, and disrupted their efforts tremendously.

'Although these sites were well defended with anti-aircraft guns, flak posed few problems after dark. They would fire at my sound, so they were usually tracking several hundred metres behind me. However, the enemy did have a dangerous weapon that was effective – radar-controlled searchlights. When turned on they could blind a pilot, leaving him unable to see his instruments. We lost a number of our aircraft to searchlights. Despite the enemy's best efforts, we were pretty effective in hindering their efforts at keeping their supply routes open.'

As 1952 came to a close, the FEAF had all but ended communist hopes of organising a serious offensive. It was now up to UN negotiators to force a truce at the bargaining table, and in order for this to happen, the fighter-bombers had to sustain the pressure that they had applied over the past seven months. This meant that the nine F-84 squadrons in-theatre would continue to fly record numbers of sorties against the main supply routes leading from Manchuria in the north to the frontline in the south.

LEFT *A 'bombed-up' 8th FBS Thunderjet taxies out from the dispersal area at K-2 to mark the start of yet another rail-cutting mission 'up north'. The large 1000-lb bomb was preferred over the '500-pounder' for this particular type of target due to the amount of destruction it caused. Granted, the smaller weapon created appreciable levels of damage, but it was found that repair crews could mend the resulting rail cuts with greater rapidity (Quinn Fuller)*

BELOW *All pilots looked forward to their jets being loaded with colourful '100 mission' bombs. The sheer volume of them present in this shot indicates that units were flying so many sorties that on some occasions several pilots might have been finishing their 100 missions on the same day. These bombs were destined for 'delivery' by pilots from the 8th FBS (Robert Paret)*

MAIN PICTURE *The crowded conditions at Taegu AB meant that resident squadrons had to park their aircraft virtually wingtip to wingtip. These Thunderjets were part of the 136th FBG, yellow-trimmed aircraft belonging to the 154th FBS and blue-trimmed jets being assigned to the 111th FBS (Charles Joseph)*

INSET LEFT *The sleek lines of Republic's F-84 are shown to good effect here with this aircraft, which is seen in the rare (for Korea at least) storeless mode. The famous 'Iron Knight' emblem decorating the nose of the aircraft denotes its assignment to the 9th FBS (Robert Fahey)*

INSET RIGHT *Most, if not all, of the original batch of F-84Es that the 182nd FBS inherited from the 27th FEW had the ANG unit's emblem painted on their respective fuselage sides. The 182nd hailed from the San Antonio area, hence the 'Eagle over the Alamo' emblem worn by the Thunderjets (J D Brown)*

OPPOSITE TOP *A 7th FBS Thunderjets simultaneously receives fuel and 0.5-in ammunition at the same time. The last crews to service the aircraft before the mission will be the 'bomb squad'. The maintenance and specialist crews put in long hours in response to the demands placed on Taegu's two Thunderjet wings by the FEAF (Leonard Guiton)*

OPPOSITE BOTTOM *This 428th FBS jet bears the scars of a ground collision with another aircraft, or vehicle, at Kunsan AB in 1952. The damage appears to be extensive, and it is not known whether the F-84 ever flew again. The two red bands on its vertical stabiliser were the trademark of the 428th (H A Gamblin)*

LEFT *Lt Colonel Gordon Blood, CO of the 49th FBG, poses by the flak damage inflicted on his aircraft whilst attacking a target during the spring of 1952. By this stage of the war, the Chinese had brought in large numbers of anti-aircraft guns, and most of their assets were well-protected. This in turn meant that F-84s suffered increasing losses as the months passed (Gordon Blood)*

TOP RIGHT *Lt Richard Merkling of the 8th FBS poses alongside a '100 mission' bomb immediately prior to flying his final mission over North Korea. Merkling rose to the rank of lieutenant general before retiring from the air force (Robert Paret)*

BOTTOM RIGHT *The entire complement of F-84s assigned to the 69th FBS are seen here neatly lined up at Taegu in the autumn of 1952. These markings had previously been used by both the 524th FES/27th FEW and the 111th FBS/136th FBG prior to the 69th arriving in-theatre. The latter unit was part of the 58th FBW (Robert Bowlin)*

OPPOSITE *Another busy day dawns for the fighter-bombers based at Taegu. Both the F-84 and the T-33 'hack' seen here belonged to the 69th FBS. This photograph was taken soon after the 58th FBW had replaced the 136th FBW in Korea in July 1952 (Roy Pitsch)*

MAIN PICTURE *The pilot of this 69th FBS Thunderjet begins his gradual let down as he crosses the 38th Parallel, and the frontline. He has expended his ordnance and is now well out of range of the MiG-15s, so all has gone well with this mission. Aside from the 69th FBS, the 310th and 311th FBSs also served as part of the 58th FBW (Robert Gilliland)*

INSET TOP LEFT *430th FBS F-84s wore some of the brightest markings in-theatre, as this recently-arrived replacement jet clearly reveals. Seen at Taegu in the autumn of 1952, it was photographed just hours after it had had the unit's distinctive yellow and black markings applied to its rear fuselage, vertical stabiliser and tip tanks (Robert Gilliland)*

INSET TOP RIGHT *Following weeks of increased combat attrition, the 49th FBG found itself reduced from 90 to just 41 aircraft by April 1952. To help redress the balance, older F-84Ds were brought in from the USA for the 136th FBW, which in turn sent its E-models aircraft to the 49th FBW. This view of the 7th FBS flightline also shows several replacement jets shipped over directly from units in America. The operational schedule of mid-1952 was so demanding that it often took weeks for the 'new' jets to be adorned with unit colours (Elliott Tours)*

INSET BOTTOM RIGHT *Despite the cold March weather, 'ordies' work on reloading 'ammo cans' into the nose of this 7th FBS F-84. Note the South Korean civilians that were hired to perform certain tasks out on the line (F I Stone)*

Engine changes became just another part of routine maintenance for all Thunderjet units in the FEAF. Indeed, by the summer of 1952, the intensity of accurate 'Triple-A' had grown to such an extent that most F-84s suffering flak damage very often had to have their engines changed upon returning to base. This aircraft is seen in pieces in the 430th FBS's maintenance area at Taegu (Robert Lines)

182nd FBS pilot J D Brown relaxes in his 'hooch' at Taegu. Privacy was a rare commodity at any of the bases in Korea, with officers typically being allocated sufficient space within a quonset hut for just a bunk bed, a desk and a footlocker or cabinet in which to secure their personal items. Due to the heavy mission load placed on the F-84 groups by the FEAF, there was very little time for pilots to relax and rest except toward the end of the war, when sufficient numbers of replacement aircrew were posted in to help ease the burden (J D Brown)

RIGHT *The 310th FBS's distinctive emblem is shown here adorning the sign that hung over the entrance to the squadron's Operations shack at Taegu. On 25 October 1952, the unit had participated in the massive strike on the 'Kumgang Political School' at Odong-ni, where over 1000 men had been trained in subversive techniques prior to infiltrating South Korea (Robert Gilliland)*

OPPOSITE TOP *This 'ditty' was posted inside the 474th FBG's Operations building at Kunsan (Cale Herry)*

OPPOSITE BOTTOM *Yet another fighter-bomber 'billboard', this time belonging to the 311th FBS at Taegu. These signs became commonplace at the various FEAF bases across South Korea, usually being posted in front of the squadrons' Operations building (Richard Ortman)*

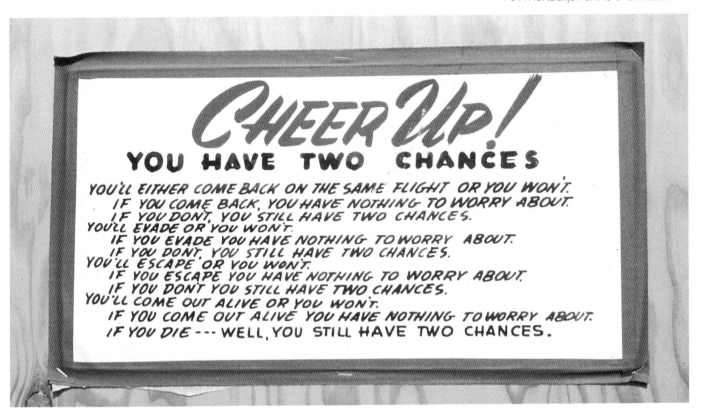

MAIN PICTURE *Fighter-bombers from the 8th FBS tuck in close as they prepare to form up with their F-86 Sabre escorts. The ensuing mission would put them within sight of the MiG base at Antung, and undoubtedly provoke a response from the resident fighter regiment. This shot was taken during the autumn of 1952 by 16th FIS Sabre pilot Lt T R White prior to the formation entering hostile airspace (T R White)*

INSET LEFT *It is late 1952, and the F-84 traffic at Taegu is heavier than ever. The various dispersal areas had been covered with PSP back in the autumn of 1950, and by this stage in the conflict it is beginning to exhibit signs of 'wear and tear'. FS-128, dubbed The Fickle Finger, was assigned to the 69th FBS, although the pace of operations at that time had prevented groundcrews from adorning the jet with full squadron colours. Indeed, only a blue circle on its vertical stabiliser identifies the F-84E as belonging to the 69th (Al Schneider)*

INSET RIGHT *7th FBS pilot Maj Robert 'Ted' Upland poses in his winter flying gear next to one of the more colourful F-84s within the 49th FBG. This photograph was taken in late 1952, towards the end of a six-month mission surge for the unit that had seen it fly 2666 combat sorties between July and December (Charles Scofield)*

MAIN PICTURE *The smoke billowing up in the background of this shot of Taegu AB was not the result of an aircraft accident, but rather a fire at the asphalt plant located on the far side of the airfield. During the first six months of 1952, the runway at the base underwent extensive lengthening and renovation, hence the need for a dedicated asphalt plant. By the time work had finished at Taegu in June 1952, the new runway had grown to 9000 ft in length. These F-84s belong to the 49th FBG (F I Stone)*

INSET TOP *Once the runway had been extended, F-84s were able to take off with two 1000-lb bombs affixed to the external pylons. Prior to this, pilots found it difficult to coax their Thunderjets into the air when fitted with just two '500 pounders' – even with the assistance of JATO. Here, a remarkably clean F-84E is mated with a 1000-lb GP bomb on the 7th FBS ramp in the autumn of 1952 (F I Stone)*

INSET BOTTOM *'Bombed up', this F-84 is heading way north into enemy territory. The tricolour markings on its vertical stabiliser, nose and tip tanks indicate that it was assigned to the CO of the 58th FBW (Al Schneider)*

CHAPTER FOUR

THE WAR WINDS DOWN

The final seven months of the war would see UN and communist ground forces locked in stalemate, with very little movement by either side. However, to achieve this impasse, the soldiers in the frontline, and the airmen in the skies above them supporting their efforts, fought a series of bloody and dangerous campaigns to keep the numerically superior Chinese and North Korean forces in check.

By early January 1953, the communists had over a million troops on Korean soil, with at least that many again held in reserve somewhere between Chienchang and Kuantien, in Manchuria. There were also more MiG-15s based at the three major airfields just north of 'MiG Alley' than ever before, and the Chinese logistics command had positioned tens of thousands of labourers along key routes to 'instantly' repair any damage done to the roads or rail links.

With this kind of infrastructure in place, should the efforts of the FEAF's fighter-bomber force be interrupted

for as little as 48 hours, the enemy forces would have had the break they needed to commence a major offensive that could have seen UN ground troops ejected from South Korea for good. To ensure that this did not happen, and effectively enforce the stalemate in the frontline that had been in place since December 1952, the Thunderjet units in-theatre maintained an exhausting operational tempo through to the ceasefire in late July 1953.

In order to fly their missions in the face of stiff MiG opposition, the fighter-bomber groups relied heavily on the support of F-86s from the 4th and 51st FIWs. Pilots from these wings achieved some spectacular successes whilst escorting F-84s south of the Yalu River, and their efforts directly resulted in numerous supply convoys (both road and rail) being destroyed.

Indeed, by early 1953 trains and trucks were the only targets still worthy of attacking with Thunderjets in North Korea, for the country's pre-war industrial base had been totally obliterated during the first months of the war in a

BELOW When looking at dateless photos of F-84s in Korea, it becomes difficult to ascertain which squadron was operating what aircraft at the time. This is because so many units simply turned their aircraft over to another squadron when they had completed their tour in Korea. For example, this jet wears the markings of the 7th FBS, but by the time this photo was taken at Taegu in June 1953, it was being flown by the 428th FBS (Milton Riggs)

series of B-29 raids. This meant that all munitions, equipment and general supplies used by the communist forces in the frontline had to be produced and shipped in from either China or the Soviet Union.

By early 1953 there were three fully-equipped F-84 groups based on Korean soil – the 49th, 58th and 474th FBGs. Within weeks, the 'ancient' F-51s and F-80s would at last be retired from the frontline, usurped by the appreciably newer, and state-of-the-art, F-86F Sabre fighter-bomber (see *Frontline Colour 2 - F-86 Sabre fighter-bomber Units over Korea* for more details). Once in service with the 8th and 18th FBWs, the Sabres proved formidable opponents for communist forces both on the ground and in the air.

Whilst the new F-86F fighter-bombers were being introduced into the FEAF, the F-84s continued to wage their own personal war against traffic travelling on the various MSRs in the north. As with the previous winters in Korea, the January weather was exceptionally bad, and although it had little overall effect on F-84 operations, heavy snows during the month did slow some of the mission surges. However, by the end of March, the 49th FBG had still managed to log almost 2600 effective sorties. The leading contributor to this outstanding effort

was the 7th FBS 'Screamin Demons', who completed a record 467 sorties during that month. Going some way to making up for the weather-affected totals of the January, this tally also exceeded the 7th's previous record figure by 37 sorties.

Whilst completing this seemingly endless cycle of missions in early 1953, Thunderjet pilots often had to battle the weather, anti-aircraft fire and MiGs. 49th FBG veteran Lt Eugene Duffy explains;

'During the winter months in early 1953, the 49th flew a wide variety of combat missions. Road reconnoitring in search of targets of opportunity were both good training missions and fun to fly. Major sorties involving multiple groups were still being flown, but targets that warranted that kind of attention were becoming harder to find. Close support missions to the frontlines were common, carrying two 500-lb bombs, 5-in rockets and napalm – armour-piercing rockets were also good tank "killers" if you could get one to fly straight and true! Most of our ammunition had been left over from World War 2, and had not been handled well.

'One morning in February, 16 of us had been briefed and were ready for a mission against what was identified as a Tank Training School, located north-east of

The 'heart and soul' of airpower's success in the Korean War was provided by the maintenance crews, rather than the pilots. The former individuals kept a large percentage of the aircraft in-theatre flying, even during the worst weather conditions imaginable. This crew chief, like most others, only took time out to sleep, shower, eat and pose for the occasional photo! 'His' aircraft was assigned to the 8th FBS at Kunsan in July 1953 (Bill Rippy)

RIGHT *A pilot from the 428th FBS shows off his freshly-painted fatigue cap. Such headwear became a tradition within the 474th FBG, and some of the artwork on display was truly outstanding. This photograph was taken after the squadron had moved from Kunsan to Taegu in early 1953 (I J Pierce)*

Pyongyang. It was not a particularly good day for bombing, with a heavy cloud base at 2000 ft and the ever-present threat of rain.

'We were scheduled for a 1000 departure, but the mission was delayed. Because of the short winter days, we rarely flew late afternoon missions to avoid the inherent risks associated with night operations in a combat zone, and a possible return with combat damage. We were expecting the mission to be cancelled when we were suddenly alerted for a 1400 take-off!

'We immediately had a problem after take-off. Clouds were forecasted to top out at 21,000 ft, with scattered layers during climb out. We took off in a combat forma-tion of four aircraft with a plan to join up on top. The violence of the turbulence we encountered during climb-out surprised me. We were totally unable to stay in flight formation and were quickly scattered. We agreed, via radio, to join up on top. When we got there, none of the other flights were in sight, and by the time we arrived over the target area, the other 12 still hadn't showed up.

'Letting down through the holes in the clouds, it didn't take long to spot our target. We made out run from east to west, hit a complex of buildings, but drew no secondary explosions. I was the last man over, and I fired my guns to make sure we got some pictures of the targets after they had been hit.

'As I pulled off the target, I noticed that the other three F-84s in my flight were a mile ahead, and already climbing into the heavy cloud layer. I fire-walled it, but knew they would be in the "soup" before I caught up. Suddenly, I noticed I was taking fire from behind! At first I thought it was ground fire, as I had failed to zig-zag off the target which was standard procedure. As I turned, I could see not one but two MiG-15s on my tail! To say I was surprised would be an understatement! MiGs coming as far south as Pyongyang was not customary, and they had caught me low, but fortunately, not slow. I was approaching 450 knots, trying to catch up with the others, so I pulled the stick straight back into my gut and headed for the cloud cover.

'For the next few minutes, I dodged in and out of cloud layers, trying to lose my pursuers. Somewhere in the "furball", one of the MiGs disappeared, leaving the other fighter to finish me off. I took several hits but none seemed to damage my ship's performance. Knowing that I had a better chance by keeping low, I "split-S'd" from about 3000 ft and popped my dive brakes to stop the wings from being ripped off the F-84. I pulled out about 300 ft off the deck and immediately started a multiple-g left turn just in time to see the MiG fly straight into the ground! I have no idea what happened to him. He was flattening out, and hit the ground directly with the belly of the aircraft and promptly exploded in a large ball of fire. I stayed in the clouds all the way back to Taegu.

'After parking my aircraft, my crew chief asked me what kind of anti-aircraft fire put all those big holes in the fuselage, and I told him it was a MiG. He did not believe me, so at that point I decided he would never believe the part about it flying into the ground. Incidentally, the crashed MiG was confirmed two days later, but I never got credit for the kill.'

ONE WING

One of the most significant events in the F-84's history in Korea occurred in early 1953 when all of the existing Thunderjet units were consolidated into one single organisation – the 58th Fighter Bomber Wing (Reinforced). Its formation came about due to the results of a study conducted between July and October 1952. All high-ranking USAF commanders in-theatre were in general agreement that a single tactical wing should contain two or more tactical groups in order to effectively, and economi-

BELOW *429th FBS pilot Lt Bill Oliphant had one of the best examples of nose-art in-theatre applied to his aircraft. 'Dennis The Menace' was the most popular cartoon character back in the 'states at the time, and Oliphant had his likeness painted onto his F-84. This shot was taken at Kunsan in the spring of 1953, right before the group moved to Taegu (Bill Oliphant)*

cally, utilise available air base facilities. Mobility of the combat groups in the forward areas was also considered a mandatory requirement.

The study had shown that a solitary wing could not operate from both a forward area base and a rear base without augmentation, whilst two groups that were equipped with identical aircraft types could consolidate their maintenance efforts at one rear base, thus eliminating the need for augmentation. By adopting the latter arrangement, only a streamlined force of specialists in various support squadrons would be needed at the forward bases.

The end result of these findings was that all existing F-84 combat groups would be placed under the control of one wing, which was officially created on 1 April 1953. The new organisation proved to be very efficient, and although it did not help generate more sorties (the F-84 squadrons were already operating to their maximum capacity), missions were both easier to plan and execute, and the support squadrons within the wing were run more effectively.

'DAMBUSTERS'

In order to force the issues being presented by the UN to the communists at the peace table, the FEAF decided to start hitting a few targets that might speed up the signing of

the ceasefire document. Up until the early spring of 1953, the big earthen dams that protected the myriad of rice paddies scattered across North Korea had been off limits to FEAF fighter-bombers due to the impact that their destruction would have on the civilian population. Some of these dams were massive in size, and had been in place for many years. Now, with the talks failing to make any progress, the FEAF was given clearance to breach them.

On 14 April the 58th FBW sent four waves of F-84s (totalling 68 aircraft) deep into North Korea to attack one of the larger earthen dams located six miles north of Sun-an, near the vital Sinanju-Pyongyang railway line. The attack was led by the wing's CO, Col Victor L Warford, and after the last aircraft had come off its bomb run, the target still appeared to be intact. The decision was made to come back the next day and hit it with everything the 58th had.

1Lt Donald Reid of the 69th FBS was on the follow-up strike;

'We launched and went up to the area where the dam was, but ran into difficulty locating it. I knew there was a big lake around there somewhere, but we couldn't see it, and for a minute I thought we were lost. Then I realised that the dam had collapsed during the night, and the lake that measured three miles long and one mile wide has disappeared! The entire valley was a mass of

mud and silt for about 12 miles, with the main rail complex being washed out in several places. We flew down low and observed that the gap in the dam was about 300 ft wide. We still had our full bomb load, so we went down the roads looking for any targets of opportunity.'

The attacks against the dams continued without let-up. Lt Randy Presley was one of the recently-arrived pilots that was flying combat missions with the 58th FBW out of Taegu AB at this time. Here, he recalls a strike that he participated in on 16 May 1953, his jet being just one of 24 F-84s (split into two sections) that were sent to attack a huge earthen dam on a 200-acre reservoir. The 58th had hit this target on the previous day, but had failed to breach it;

'This was a real dilly of a mission. We were sending 24 of our aircraft against the same dam for the second straight day. Instead of bombing from west to east, we orbited and then hit it from the opposite direction. The first 12 came in from the back side and our section came in from the water side. Since there was supposedly no flak in the area according to the briefing, I bore on down at a much lower altitude than I should have so as to get the pipper right on the water line. I don't remember seeing Lt Davis drop his bombs, and just as I pulled off, and as my nose was coming through the horizon, something blew

OPPOSITE Lt Bob Lines shows off his new 'poopy suit' which all pilots were required to wear during the long winter missions. If he had been shot down over the sea, it would have given him a slim chance of survival in the freezing waters off the Korean coast (Robert Lines)

BELOW Numerically, the most impressive array of F-84s ever seen in Korea was to be found at Taegu in the late spring of 1953. The formation of the 58th FBW(Reinforced) came about due to the consolidation of several Thunderjet squadrons, and it was this reorganisation that made identification of aircraft so difficult. The black and yellow-tailed aircraft seen here had previously been operated by the 8th FBS/49th FBG, but by July 1953 it was being flown by the 429th FBS – although its markings had not changed one single bit! (Otto Kopf)

me over on my back and I was looking *up* at the rice paddies!

'I didn't say anything because I was sure that Davis's bombs (we were using seven- and ten-second delayed action fuses) had gone off under me and flipped me over. I had a gaping hole in the left wing, with about 35 per cent of the inboard left aileron blown off. Lt Davis turned around and joined up with me, making a visual inspection, after which he said I was not losing any fluids and everything looked okay – with the exception of the big hole in my wing.

'We flew out to the west coast of North Korea and turned south, following the coastline back to Seoul (K-13). I asked him to stay at around 200 mph because the aluminium that had peeled back on top of the wing was flapping wildly. All of the gauges on my instrument panel looked fine. We chose Seoul over Kimpo to land because of the longer runway. I pulled off an uneventful landed without flaps.

'After getting out and inspecting my aircraft, I found that there were close to 200 holes in the left aft fuselage area and a further 15 in the vertical stabiliser. The jet had really taken a beating on the underside. I was lucky to have been able to fly it back in one piece.'

The official history of the 58th FBW contains the following statistics pertaining to targets attacked between 13 and 16 May 1953. The initial strikes on several large earthen dams began on the former date when 59 Thunderjets breached the 2300-foot-long Toksan Dam. The resulting deluge washed six miles of railroad embankment and five bridges downstream, whilst the force of the water also destroyed several hundred buildings and ruined five square miles of rice crops.

Buoyed by this success, FEAF commander, Lt-Gen Otto P Weyland, scheduled strikes on a further two dams. It was on the 16th that the 58th attacked the Chasan Dam as previously related by Lt Presley. The final wave of Thunderjets to hit the target scored a cluster of

BELOW *Ready for war, the 8th FBS's* Thunder Mug *waits for its pilot to emerge from the mission briefing hut at Taegu. The 'ordnance of the day' appears to be two 500-lb GP bombs, four 5-in HVARs and the standard load of 0.5-in ammunition. The 8th had been in action since 1950, when it rushed its F-80Cs into Korea from Ashiya AB, in Japan. The unit's first base in-theatre was Taegu, where it remained until the 49th FBG moved to Kunsan in April 1953 (Lynn Balow)*

five direct hits, and the pressure created by the bombs bursting underwater split the dam apart. At the end of the war, Lt-Gen Weyland commented that that there were two particular fighter-bomber strikes that proved to be 'spectacular'. One was the massive air strike against the hydro-electric plants in June 1952, and the other was the 'taking out' of the earthen dams in May 1953. In both of these well executed attacks, it was the numerically superior F-84s that dropped the bulk of the bombs that destroyed these vital communist assets.

SUIHO DAM

If you were to study the records of 50 Thunderjet pilots that flew over Korea during the 1952-53 period, you find that all of them went after one specific target more times than any other – the Suiho Dam. The most important hydro-electric installation in Korea, this dam was also the fourth largest of its type in the world. Built over 12 years by the Japanese Nitrogenous Fertiliser Company in the 1930s and 40s, it straddled the Yalu River some 30 miles north-east of Antung, in Manchuria. It was 349 feet high and 2950 feet wide.

When the B-29s levelled the industrial heartland of North Korea in the autumn of 1950, it was decided that attacking these electric power facilities served no great military purpose, so they were bypassed. But in 1952 UN intelligence sources discovered that much of North Korea's war production infrastructure had been rebuilt underground, and that it was relying on power from these hydro-electric plants. The dams now became prime targets. Needless to say, the Suiho complex was number one on the list of assets to be protected by the swarming MiG-15s that were based across the Yalu at Antung and Mukden.

Lt Leland S Speakes of the 430th FBS/474th BG was one of the many F-84 pilots tasked with bombing this well-defended target. He recounts a typical mission;

'It was sometime early in 1953 that this strike was flown. It was one of those "hush-hush" missions, and we got up very early for the briefing. There were 17 pilots selected for the strike, with 16 F-84Gs comprising the main force – the extra jet would get airborne as a spare in case of any aborts during the early stages of the mission.

'The pre-flight briefing was much the same as usual, except for the warning that this target was the most heavily fortified in all of North Korea, and that we would be extremely lucky if all of us got in and off the target

ABOVE *A group of seasoned Thunderjet pilots enjoy a few minutes of down-time out on the flightline. Wearing his distinctive Royal Air Force-issue grey flying overall, exchange pilot Nigel Bayne tinkers with his camera. These men were all assigned to the 429th FBS at Kunsan (K-8), its controlling 474th FBG sharing this base on the west coast of South Korea with another USAF group and a squadron of Marine nightfighters (Bill Oliphant)*

Three more veteran Thunderjet pilots from the 429th FBS pose alongside a well-worn F-84E at Taegu prior to flying yet another bombing mission. Lts Kopf, Armstrong and Walker were photographed just days before the 27 July 1953 ceasefire brought an end to the Korean War (Otto Kopf)

RIGHT *Quite a number of RAF pilots completed exchange tours with the F-84 and F-86 squadrons in Korea. They impressed their hosts both in the air and on the ground, thanks to their flying abilities when in the cockpit, and socialising skills when out of it! Now seen wearing his 'battle dress blues', Nigel Bayne enjoys a spot of liquid refreshment with his crew chief at Kunsan during the spring of 1953 (Bill Oliphant)*

without suffering battle damage. Flying as the "spare", I felt sure that I would not get a chance to continue the mission because the primary aircraft usually worked just fine. However, even before all of the F-84s had taken off, one pilot called in to report that his engine fire warning light was on, so I slid into his place in the formation.

'We were each carrying two 500-lb GP bombs with delayed fuses. As I pulled the nose up, I was thinking that we would have a good chance to mix it up with MiG-15s down at low altitude. We climbed up to 35,000 ft, levelled off, and manoeuvred into battle formation.

'The sky was clear and it was a great day to be flying. We made the usual radio checks and radar verifications as we crossed over the frontlines into North Korea. Because of the anticipated heavy flak, and the chance of encountering enemy fighters, we started letting down shortly after passing Pyongyang. By the time we got close to the Suiho Dam, we would be down on the deck, which made it harder for the MiGs to blindside us. We dropped into trail formation and flew up the river until right before us was a huge dam every bit as big as those "out west" in the US.

'There were six generator houses in the complex, and those were our targets. I was the last of the 16 aeroplanes, so I was in a position to observe where all the bombs had gone, and what damage they had caused. Most of the bombs hit that concrete dam and bounced off like basketballs! What a sight! Several of them entered the generator houses and didn't come out, which was exactly what we wanted.

'I had seen a lot of anti-aircraft fire over Pyongyang, but never anything like the flak we encountered over Suiho. It was so thick that almost every square inch had some type of burst going off. I didn't see how any aircraft could penetrate that, hit the target and get out in one piece! We all dropped our bombs as precisely as possible, and our only thought was to get the hell out of there!

'As I came off the target it felt like they had me locked in pretty good. I could feel the concussion from those big black AAA shells, and there was no doubt in my mind that I was probably hit bad. We had briefed that the leader was going to come off his bomb run at about 96 per cent power so we could all catch up. However, when I came off the run, I looked out in front of me and there wasn't an aircraft in sight – just some faint streams of black smoke from planes that had been pulling 100 per cent power trying to get out of the area!

'At this point I had climbed back up to 20,000 ft, and after checking all my gauges, I glanced out of the cockpit to visually check for any damage. When I looked to the right, sitting on my wing was a MiG-15! It was bright and shiny, and didn't have writing all over it like our aircraft did. On the side of the fuselage was a big red star. He had obviously pulled a pursuit curve on me, and the entire nose of the MiG was black with gun smoke. By some miracle he had missed me, and I could see him sitting in the cockpit looking just as scared as I did!

'I immediately turned into him with all the strength that I could muster, and he disappeared under my tail. I turned 90 degrees and then turned back, and there he

BELOW *A newly-delivered replacement F-84 basks in the spring sunshine at Kimpo (K-14), having only recently been adorned with the colours of the 9th FBS. Quite why it was visiting this base has not been recorded, as Kimpo was then home to the 4th FIW and the 67th Tactical Reconnaissance Wing (Stanley Newman)*

RIGHT *A member of the 69th FBS's 'bomb squad' eases a '1000 pounder' off the delivery truck and onto the bomb jack that will place the weapon in position under the F-84's wing pylon. These crews were kept constantly busy 'feeding' fighter-bombers with bombs, rockets, napalm and belted machine gun rounds to expend against targets travelling along the main supply routes during* Operation Strangle *(Roy Pitsch)*

OPPOSITE *As the war ground on, so the number of mobile AAA batteries increased, backed up by small arms fire from communist troops under attack. Although most F-84s returned to base without as much as a scratch, some limped home badly shot up. Falling into the latter category, the aircraft that this shattered windscreen belonged to hailed from the 428th FBS. The jet 'caught' a 20 mm round dead in the centre of the Plexiglas windscreen whilst in the final stages a dive-bombing run. And although the cannon shell did not penetrate the Plexiglas, it ruined the line of vision for the pilot, and forced groundcrews at K-8 to replace the screen prior to the jet flying its next mission (Cale Herry)*

ABOVE *Most F-84s that flew in the Korean War had names painted on both sides of the cockpit, and a few also boasted colourful nose-art. This photograph was taken when the 'artist' from the 429th FBS was still in the early stages of creating his latest 'aluminium masterpiece' (Doug Iverson)*

was right in my gunsights. I pulled the trigger and did not release it until every round had been fired. I saw several hits on his aircraft, but none caused a fire or explosion. He rapidly disappeared to the north and I headed home, almost out of fuel.

'When I got back to base and attended the debriefing, we were all excited about the good job we had done on the target. Our flight leader on this occasion had been Ed Izor, who had served as a World War 2 bomber pilot and attacked the Ploesti Oil Refineries. He said the flak was heavier at Suiho than back then! All of our F-84s returned safely, and as a result of the damage we had done, we were all awarded the Distinguished Flying Cross.'

During the tens of thousands of sorties that F-84 pilots flew over North Korea, they quickly became adept at keeping their target in sight and their tail clear of MiGs.

Despite often flying under the umbrella of dedicated F-86 top cover, there was never any reason for Thunderjet pilots to relax their guard, for the large formations of enemy fighters would occasionally penetrate the Sabre formations.

Although fighter-bomber pilots were left in no doubt as to the intentions of their communist foe, they often wondered about the nationality of the men in the cockpit of the MiGs they encountered. 69th FBS pilot Lt Roy Pitsch remembers;

'We flew several missions against the big dam on the Yalu. We were always supposed to knock out the power-plants and leave the dam itself intact. I guess we did a good job of it, but the dam did take a few hard hits.

'It got to be a bit exciting though, as we could see all those MiG-15s taking off across the river. That area was strictly "off limits" to any of our aircraft, so there was

LEFT *A clear view of the instrument panel and general cockpit layout of the F-84E. Although it may look fairly complicated to those unfamiliar with the art of fast jet flying, FEAF pilots rated the Thunderjet's 'office' user-friendly. This aircraft belonged to the 7th FBS 'Screamin Demons' (Leonard Guiton)*

nothing we could do about it. On one mission, as I was pulling off the target after dropping my "500 pounders", a MiG crossed right in front of me and I shot off a few rounds at it, but at that angle-off it was impossible to draw enough lead to score. I did get a picture with my gun camera though, and the film was hustled off to Tokyo for analysis. I never did hear if there was anything on it worth looking at, however. We had always heard tales, mostly from the interceptor guys, about MiG pilots with blond or red hair. It sure made us wonder about who was behind the stick?'

The relentless pressure put on the Chinese re-supply efforts during the spring finally resulted in the ceasefire of late July 1953. The principal USAF types responsible for the destruction of rolling stock and railway track during the closing months of the war were the F-84, F-86F and the nightflying B-26. The marines and navy also flew their fair share of missions with their F9F Panthers and AD Skyraiders.

As the days ticked by until the truce was implemented on 27 July, the communists frantically tried to repair their North Korean airfields so that they could recover aircraft. The primary reason for this was that when the truce came into effect, both sides would only be allowed to keep those aircraft in-theatre that were already on Korean soil at that time – no additional squadrons could move in after the ceasefire. All airfields in

North Korea were immediately moved to the top of the priority 'hit' list!

GROUND SUPPORT MISSIONS

The months of May, June and July also saw a greater emphasis placed on the ground support tasking. This came about primarily because communist forces had launched a series of renewed attacks on UN positions during the last week of June. The Chinese and North Korean armies would maintain this pressure along the frontline until the very moment the truce was actually signed.

In response to this renewed aggression, both the 58th and 474th FBGs completed no less than 2207 close support sorties during the last month of the war. And this was despite the fact that for the final 27 days of the conflict the (reinforced) wing was only able to fly on 23 of them.

The last fighter-bomber sorties of the war were completed by the 58th FBW. At 1730 on 27 July (four-and-a-half hours after Gen Mark W Clark had signed the ceasefire document), Col Joseph Davis Jr, commanding officer of the wing, led 24 Thunderjets on one of the deepest fighter-bomber penetrations of the war. The mission saw the jets attack Lin-Chiang airfield, which was situated just one solitary mile short of the Manchurian border.

BELOW *An excellent overall view of Lt Bill Oliphant's* **THE MENACE,** *which was part of the 429th FBS at Kunsan AB during the early spring of 1953. Soon after this photograph was taken, the 474th FBG became part of the 58th FBW (Reinforced)* *(William Oliphant)*

This base received unparalleled attention during the final hours of the war, for UN intelligence sources believed that the Chinese would try to fly MiGs in if they could make the runway serviceable. Davis's aircraft were loaded with 500-lb GP bombs, and his pilots cratered the runway with 12 tons of explosives. By the time the F-84s returned to base, the sun had set and the aircraft had only minutes of fuel left.

The last four jets over the target were flown by the following pilots – Lt Carl S Miller (430th FBS) Lt I J 'Pete' Pierce (428th FBS), Lt Chester C Lamb (430th FBS) and Lt Otto R Kopf (429th FBS). These men had dropped the last bombs expended by the F-84 in Korea.

After the war, surviving Thunderjets remained in service with both the USAF and the ANG well into the late 1950s, whilst many G-models were handed over to the Nationalist Chinese Air Force.

Despite the straight-winged F-84 being considered obsolete almost as soon as it had entered series production in early 1947, the Thunderjet carved for itself a role in a war that no one could have predicted when the first examples were rolled out of the Farmingdale plant. Almost five decades later, those surviving fighter-bomber pilots that braved both flak and fighters in the F-84 still have fond memories of Republic's 'ground-loving hog'.

ABOVE *None of the fighter-bomber squadrons that participated in the Korean War ever let the 100th mission of a pilot go by without celebrating such an important personal milestone. This photograph was taken when the 428th FBS's Lt Taylor became a 'centurion'. At around the same time the unit was renumbered the 7th FBS. Note the proliferation of instructional stencilling on the stores pylon (Randy Presley)*

428TH FIGHTER BOMBER
FS-428
SQUADRON
CAUTION
BEWARE
OF JET
BLAST

OPPOSITE This 428th FBS sign was posted by their Operations shack at Taegu AB in the early summer of 1953. By then, the squadron had been incorporated into the 58th FBW (Reinforced), having previously been under the command of the 474th FBG (I J Pierce)

LEFT The convoy of trolleys hauling bombs from the ammunition dump to the flightline was seemingly endless. Some days, armourers would have to load well over 100 bombs onto jets, in addition to the napalm, rockets and 0.5-in 'ammo'. Ordnance was always stored and prepared well away from the flightline (Rudy Danbom)

BELOW LEFT 58th FBW commanding officer Col Joseph Davis poses alongside his Thunderjet. The tricolour scheme worn by the aircraft represents all three squadrons within the wing, namely the 69th, 310th and 311th FBSs. Due to the paucity of F-84s in-theatre, and the 58th's intense mission cycle, the colonel's aircraft was flown by a number of pilots including himself (Jack Marsh)

OPPOSITE TOP *Lt Don James poses beside his 8th FBS Thunderjet HOOSIER HOTSHOT. This aircraft also boasts the unit's famous 'Black Sheep' badge on its nose, despite the emblem not being officially approved until 1960! Today, the squadron flies F-117A stealth fighters adorned with the same emblem (Don James)*

OPPOSITE BOTTOM *This 8th FBS F-84 carries the unusual combination of two 100-lb bombs under each wing and single '1000 pounders' on each of the wingroot pylons. Finally, a solitary JATO bottle is also visible beneath the national marking (Robert Paret)*

LEFT TOP *Lt Pete Orr had the honour of flying his 100th mission in the wing CO's Thunderjet. Note that the two 1000-lb bombs have already received their special '100 mission' paint schemes, courtesy of the squadron armourers. The 58th FBW was headquartered at Taegu at this time. When the newly-lengthened 9000-ft runway became operational at the base in June 1952, it at last meant that F-84s could carry these larger bombs (Pete Orr)*

LEFT BOTTOM *These 429th FBS F-84s are being prepared for yet another mission out of Kunsan. Note the variations in the tail and tip tank markings – blue bands denote aircraft belonging to the 429th, whilst the remaining jets are replacements F-84s from other units. This shot was taken in the spring of 1953 (Doug Iverson)*

Having completed the mission brief, pilots from the 311th FBS have piled out of the Operations hut and clambered aboard either a covered GMC truck or a drop-sided trailer, hitched to a ubiquitous Jeep. They would then be driven the short distance to the flightline at Taegu, where bombed-up Thunderjets awaited their arrival. This photograph was taken in early 1953, by which time sufficient numbers of F-86s were available in-theatre to ward off the MiG-15 threat, and allow these pilots to concentrate on their targets (Gene Rohr)

ABOVE *Although the end of the war was just days away, the flow of replacement aircraft into Korea from Japan did not let up. This new F-84G was photographed during one such ferry flight to Taegu AB, where it was to be issued to the 58th FBW (Reinforced). Note the two long-range external fuel tanks fitted to the wing root pylons especially for this flight. After the war, some of the newer G-models in Korea were flown to Formosa (now Taiwan) for service with the Nationalist Chinese Air Force (Milton Riggs)*

RIGHT *The lineage of the 8th FBS dates all the way back to November 1940. During World War, it flew four different frontline fighters, namely the P-40, P-47, P-38 and P-51. In Korea War, the unit saw action flying both the the F-80 and F-84. This sign was posted outside the squadron bar at Kunsan in 1953 (Bill Rippy)*

LEFT *During the last few months of the war, F-84s from the 428th and 429th FBSs began displaying some of the most elaborate nose-art of the entire war. Most of it was inspired by the female form, like this example painted onto a jet from the 428th FBS. Only a few photos exist of such artwork, and they were all taken in the spring of 1953, suggesting that the nose-art was removed soon after the ceasefire came into effect (Bill Boland)*

BELOW *Lt Leland Speakes gives the photographer a thumb's up as he taxies out of the dispersal area. Note the 430th FBS emblem painted on the right side of his aircraft. This photograph was taken in early 1953 at Kunsan AB (Leland Speakes)*

This 182nd FBS F-84 was shot up so badly over North Korea that it could not make it back to Taegu, its pilot having to carry out a wheels-up landing at Suwon (K-13) instead. Maintenance personnel were flown in hours later and the aircraft sufficiently patched up to allow it to be flown back to base under its own 'steam'. Once at Taegu, it was fully repaired and returned to the regular mission rotation. Parked behind the F-84 at K-13 is a sorry-looking F-80C, which seems to be surrounded by the various 'bits' that were broken off when it crash-landed (Ed Garnett)

ABOVE *Slipping down below the remaining members of his flight, Lt Milton Riggs took this photograph soon after the pilots had joined up to head south after completing a combat mission over North Korea – note that all the F-84s have dropped their bombs. The blue markings denote that these jets are from the 69th FBS (Milton Riggs)*

RIGHT *Pilot Rudy Danbom proves that the weather had to be pretty bad to slow down F-84 operations. The fresh snow that has piled up during the night will be cleaned off, and the aircraft, already prepped for the next mission, duly cleared for take-off. This wintry shot was taken on the 7th FBS's flightline at K-2 in early 1953 (Rudy Danbom)*

LEFT *The prominent red and white chevrons on these F-84s leave no doubt as to which squadron is flying them – the 'Iron Knights' of the 9th FBS. Aside from the tail and tip tank markings, the unit also painted its emblem on the nose of each of its aircraft. This tradition had started with the F-80s that the 9th had flown during the early stages of the Korean War. (Arnold Braswell)*

BELOW *With the Chinese trying to stockpile supplies in order to support one huge offensive before the ceasefire, armourers tasked with turning around jets between strike missions had to load bombs, rockets and 'ammo' in the shortest possible time. This 429th FBG F-84G, seen at Taegu, will launch with two of these 1000-lb bombs on its next mission (Otto Kopf)*

RIGHT *Lt Wes Jacobson is seen flying the wing commander's Thunderjet during a Rescap mission deep into North Korea. Aside from its distinctive tricolour markings, the aircraft also wears the 430th FBS badge below its cockpit. The large centreline tank is filled with survival gear to be dropped to the downed pilot. Its contents would help him survive until a helicopter could be flown into the area to winch him to safety. Retrieving pilots that had been shot down over enemy territory was never easy (Wes Jacobson)*

BELOW *8th FBS pilots have finished their briefing, made the ride to the flightline, strapped into their jets and started their engines. This squadron-strength strike will call for 1000-lb bombs to be delivered against specified targets in North Korea. Typically, the larger ordnance was used to disable key rail centres, or to make rail cuts in areas that would prove hard for repair crews to access. This shot was taken in the spring of 1953 at Taegu AB (Quinn Fuller)*

OPPOSITE *Three pilots from the 429th FBS vacate their briefing hut and stroll out to the flightline at Kunsan. The weather for the day's mission is clear, but bitterly cold. The 474th FBG shared the base with the 3rd Bomb Wing (B-26s) and VMF(N)-513 (F3Ds), who provided night protection for B-29s that were bombing targets along the Yalu River (Bill Oliphant)*

RIGHT *The weather in Korea in the spring of 1953 was wet and muddy, but it had little effect on UN air efforts aimed at restricting the movement of communist supplies to the south. PSP made it easier for jets to taxy around, but as can be seen here, conditions were on the whole pretty miserable. This 429th FBS F-84 is being loaded with two 1000-lb 'blockbuster' bombs, which was the aircraft's maximum permissible load (Bill Oliphant)*

BELOW *By the end of 1952, servicing facilities for the F-84 at Taegu AB had improved to such an extent that most major maintenance could be carried out in a protected environment. This jet is seen undergoing an engine change after suffering heavy battle damage during a mission flown in the early summer of 1953 (Jack Marsh)*

ABOVE This 429th FBS F-84 is being serviced, loaded and turned around in double-quick time at Kunsan in early 1953. The bomb truck has just off loaded two 1000-lb 'blockbuster' bombs that will be uploaded by the ordnance crews. In the background are B-26s from the 3rd BW (Doug Iverson)

LEFT This 7th FBS F-84G was powered by a J35-A-29 engine, which allowed the jet to achieve speeds of close to 600 mph (clean) in level flight. However, when loaded with ordnance, it was not wise to 'pull' 100 per cent power unless you were trying to get away from a MiG-15. Engine changes were usually performed in the open at forward bases (John Glanton)

Lt Quint Fuller poses alongside his EL TIGRE at Taegu AB in early 1953. He was assigned to the 8th FBS, which in turn became the 429th FBS following the 474th FBG's assignment to to the 58th FBW (Reinforced). Despite the redesignation, the unit retained its bright yellow nose and tail trim on its F-84s. All Thunderjet operations in Korea were based out of K-2 by this late stage of the war (Quint Fuller)

Appendices

F-84 THUNDERJET UNITS IN KOREA

27th FEW

522nd FES
523rd FES
524th FES

Part of Strategic Air Command, the 27th FEW was based at Bergstrom AFB, Texas, prior to moving to the Far East. It flew combat missions out of Itazuke AB, Japan, and Taegu AB, Korea. In May 1951 it was relieved by the ANG-manned 136th FBG, which in turn took over the 27th's aircraft and kept its squadron markings.

136th FBG

111th FBS
154th FBS
182nd FBS

An ANG wing comprised of units drawn from Texas and Arkansas, this group flew out of Taegu AB until early July 1952. It was then relieved by the 58th FBW. As with the 136th before it, the 58th in turn used the same aircraft as its predecessors, retaining the same squadron markings.

49th FBG

7th FBS
8th FBS
9th FBS

This group saw combat for the entire duration of the Korean War, initially in F-80Cs. In the spring of 1951, it replaced its Shooting Stars with F-84Es, which the group would operate until war's end in July 1953. The 49th FBG's Thunderjets were identified by bold chevrons painted on the vertical stabiliser and tip tanks. In April 1953 the group moved from its long-term base at Taegu to Kunsan.

474th FBG

428th FBS
429th FBS
430th FBS

Activated on 10 July 1952, the 474th replaced the ANG-manned 116th FBW within the FEAF. Four days later it relocated to Kunsan AB (K-8), and flew its first combat missions on 1 August. The 474th operated from K-8 until April 1953, at which time the group moved to Taegu AB to become part of the 58th FBW (Reinforced).

58th FBW

69th FBS
310th FBS
311th FBS

The wing was reactivated on 10 July 1952 to replace the 136th FBG at Taegu AB. Remaining in-theatre through to the ceasefire, it continued to fly Thunderjets in South Korea postwar until transitioning to the F-86F Sabre and moving to Osan AB.

116th FBW

158th FBS
159th FBS
195th FBS

An ANG wing called to active duty during the autumn of 1950, the 116th was sent to the Far East principally to bolster the air defences of Japan. The wing did not have a regular operational base on Korean soil, but did fly numerous bombing missions out of Taegu. The 116th was also involved in the development of tactical aerial refuelling while in-theatre. Its assignment to the FEAF ended in July 1952.

CONFIRMED F-84 THUNDERJET AIR-TO-AIR KILLS IN KOREA

Pilot	Squadron	Date	Aircraft Destroyed
Lt Col William Bertram	523rd FES	21/1/51	MiG-15
Capt William Slaughter	522nd FES	23/1/51	MiG-15
1Lt Jacob Kratt	523rd FES	23/1/51	MiG-15 (x 2)
1Lt Jacob Kratt	523rd FES	26/1/51	Yak-3
1Lt Arthur Oligher	182nd FBS	26/6/51	MiG-15 (.5)
Capt Harry Underwood	182nd FBS	26/6/51	MiG-15 (.5)
Capt Kenneth Skeen	9th FBS	19/9/51	MiG-15
1Lt Farris Fortner	154th FBS	23/10/51	MiG-15
Lt(jg) Walter Schirra	154th FBS	23/10/51	MiG-15
1Lt Kenneth Cooley	111th FBS	18/11/51	MiG-15 (.5)
1Lt John Hewett	111th FBS	18/11/51	MiG-15 (.5)
Capt Paul Mitchell	158th FBS	15/12/51	MiG-15

REPUBLIC F-84G THUNDERJET

Powerplant

Allison J35-A-29 axial-flow turbojet, rated at 5600 lb (2540 kg) thrust

Fuel

Internal fuel capacity, 376 Imp gal (1709 l), with provision for two wingtip and two underwing 191.5 Imp gal (870 l) drop tanks

Performance

- Max speed, 622 mph (1001 km/h) at sea level
- 575 mph (925 km/h) at 20,000 ft (6095 m)
- 510 mph (869 km/h) at 36,000 ft (10,970 m)
Continuous cruise - 483 mph (777 km/h) at 35,000 ft (10,670 m)
Time to 35,000 ft (10,670 m) - 7.9 min, and 9.4 min with external tanks
Service ceiling - 40,500 ft (12,345 m)
Range - internal fuel, 670 miles (1078 km), with wingtip tanks 1330 miles (2140 km), and with maximum external fuel 2000 miles (3217 km)

Weights

Empty - 11,095 lb (5033 kg)
Normal loaded - 18,645 lb (8457 kg)
Maximum load - 23,525 lb (10,670 kg)

Dimensions

Span - 36 ft 5 in (11.09 m)
Length - 38 ft 1 in (11.60 m)
Height - 12 ft 7 in (3.83 m)
Wing area - 260 sq ft (24.25 m²)

Armament

Six 0.5-in (12.7 mm) Colt-Browning M-3 machine-guns, with 300 rounds per gun, and provision for up to 4000-lb (1184-kg) of external ordnance, including 100-, 500- and 1000-lb GP bombs, napalm and 'Tiny Tim' 30-cm and 5-in HVARs

Republic F-84G Thunderjet

29 Rudder pedals
30 Instrument panel
31 Control column
32 Instrument panel shroud
33 Sperry radar gunsight
34 Bullet-proof windscreen
35 Cockpit canopy cover
36 Canopy framing
37 Starboard side console panel
38 Pilot's ejection seat
39 Engine throttle control

1 Engine air intake
2 Gun laying radar seeker
3 Machine gun muzzles
4 Pitot tube
5 Main undercarriage leg strut
6 Steering control
7 Nosewheel
8 Shimmy damper
9 Taxying lamp
10 Nosewheel retraction strut
11 Nosewheel doors
12 Bifurcated intake ducting
13 Nosewheel hydraulic retraction jack
14 Machine gun barrels
15 Gyro compass unit
16 Ballast weights
17 Ammunition tanks (300 rounds per gun)
18 M-3 0.5-in (12.7 mm) machine guns
19 Spent cartridge case collector chute
20 Nosewheel bay between intake ducts
21 Battery
22 Servicing access panels
23 Gun bay access panel latch
24 Oxygen converter
25 Hydraulic system header tank
26 Gun bay access panel
27 Armoured bulkhead
28 Cockpit front pressure bulkhead

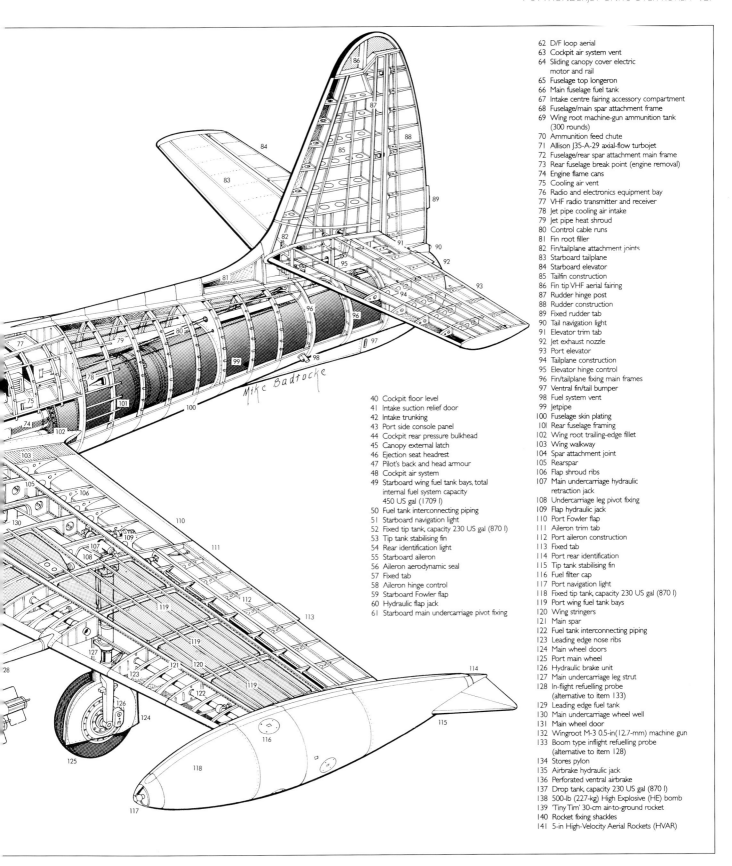

62 D/F loop aerial
63 Cockpit air system vent
64 Sliding canopy cover electric
motor and rail
65 Fuselage top longeron
66 Main fuselage fuel tank
67 Intake centre fairing accessory compartment
68 Fuselage/main spar attachment frame
69 Wing root machine-gun ammunition tank
(300 rounds)
70 Ammunition feed chute
71 Allison J35-A-29 axial-flow turbojet
72 Fuselage/rear spar attachment main frame
73 Rear fuselage break point (engine removal)
74 Engine flame cans
75 Cooling air vent
76 Radio and electronics equipment bay
77 VHF radio transmitter and receiver
78 Jet pipe cooling air intake
79 Jet pipe heat shroud
80 Control cable runs
81 Fin root filler
82 Fin/tailplane attachment joints
83 Starboard tailplane
84 Starboard elevator
85 Tailfin construction
86 Fin tip VHF aerial fairing
87 Rudder hinge post
88 Rudder construction
89 Fixed rudder tab
90 Tail navigation light
91 Elevator trim tab
92 Jet exhaust nozzle
93 Port elevator
94 Tailplane construction
95 Elevator hinge control
96 Fin/tailplane fixing main frames
97 Ventral fin/tail bumper
98 Fuel system vent
99 Jetpipe
100 Fuselage skin plating
101 Rear fuselage framing
102 Wing root trailing-edge fillet
103 Wing walkway
104 Spar attachment joint
105 Rearspar
106 Flap shroud ribs
107 Main undercarriage hydraulic
retraction jack
108 Undercarriage leg pivot fixing
109 Flap hydraulic jack
110 Port Fowler flap
111 Aileron trim tab
112 Port aileron construction
113 Fixed tab
114 Port rear identification
115 Tip tank stabilising fin
116 Fuel filter cap
117 Port navigation light
118 Fixed tip tank, capacity 230 US gal (870 l)
119 Port wing fuel tank bays
120 Wing stringers
121 Main spar
122 Fuel tank interconnecting piping
123 Leading edge nose ribs
124 Main wheel doors
125 Port main wheel
126 Hydraulic brake unit
127 Main undercarriage leg strut
128 In-flight refuelling probe
(alternative to item 133)
129 Leading edge fuel tank
130 Main undercarriage wheel well
131 Main wheel door
132 Wingroot M-3 0.5-in (12.7-mm) machine gun
133 Boom type inflight refuelling probe
(alternative to item 128)
134 Stores pylon
135 Airbrake hydraulic jack
136 Perforated ventral airbrake
137 Drop tank, capacity 230 US gal (870 l)
138 500-lb (227-kg) High Explosive (HE) bomb
139 'Tiny Tim' 30-cm air-to-ground rocket
140 Rocket fixing shackles
141 5-in High-Velocity Aerial Rockets (HVAR)

40 Cockpit floor level
41 Intake suction relief door
42 Intake trunking
43 Port side console panel
44 Cockpit rear pressure bulkhead
45 Canopy external latch
46 Ejection seat headrest
47 Pilot's back and head armour
48 Cockpit air system
49 Starboard wing fuel tank bays, total
internal fuel system capacity
450 US gal (1709 l)
50 Fuel tank interconnecting piping
51 Starboard navigation light
52 Fixed tip tank, capacity 230 US gal (870 l)
53 Tip tank stabilising fin
54 Rear identification light
55 Starboard aileron
56 Aileron aerodynamic seal
57 Fixed tab
58 Aileron hinge control
59 Starboard Fowler flap
60 Hydraulic flap jack
61 Starboard main undercarriage pivot fixing

Mike Badrocke

F-84 Thunderjet Patch Gallery